From Farms to Arms

The History of Catterick Military Training Area

Edited by Nancy Tanner and Phil Abramson
With assistance from Josephine Haskett

Safety and Visitors to Catterick Training Area

Visitors to Catterick Training Area are reminded that they are accessing land owned by the Ministry of Defence (MoD) that is used for military training. The land may also be managed by an agricultural tenant.

Whilst the MoD has a presumption in favour of public access where compatible with public safety, conservation and the interest of its tenants, access may be denied due to safety, operational or training requirements.

No access should be attempted when Red warning flags or lanterns are displayed as live firing is in progress.

For further information regarding public access or if in any doubt contact Range Control on 01748 875503 or 01830 520569, or the Security and Public Access Officer, DIO Training North, Wathgill Camp, Downholme, Richmond, North Yorkshire, DL11 6AH.

Contents

Cover photograph: Home Guard in Downholme, c.1940s. Resident Michael Webster in uniform on Silver Street.
(Courtesy of Mrs D. West)

Foreword

Lieutenant Colonel Mark Holden
Commander, Service Delivery Training North

It is 100 years since the outbreak of the Great War, when it was quickly understood that the small peacetime British Army would need to expand rapidly if it was to meet the very real threat of a large-scale conflict that was being fought on an industrial scale by large standing armies. When, in 1914 the War Department identified Catterick and its surrounding countryside as suitable for military training to meet this need, they may not have foreseen the enduring importance of Catterick Training Area in training future generations of soldiers. It is soldiers trained at Catterick who have defended the Nation and fought its wars, large and small for over a century. From Kitchener's Volunteers of 1914 and 1915, the Armoured and Artillery Crews of the Second World War, the Signallers of the Cold War and latterly a generation of Infantrymen who have fought the small wars of the late 20th and early 21st Century, Catterick's rugged countryside and austere weather have

been pivotal in forging military capability. But the Training Area does not exist in isolation. It is a complex environment of farmland that is managed by hard-working families, many of whom have been on the land for generations. It contains scientific, environmental and historically important sites that have to be managed around increasingly complex and demanding training needs and it is a haven for many rare species of plants and animals. This book is an insight to Catterick Training Area and its many facets. It is a testament to all those who have trained over its terrain, farmed its land and managed its sites of historical and environmental importance. This book has been produced by a team of dedicated volunteers who deserve our thanks for capturing in writing and pictures the diversity of activity on this unique training area.

Introduction

"Most military training areas are in remote unspoiled parts of the country. It is our duty to preserve such land for the future by guarding most carefully against misuse or mismanagement. One such area is Catterick and Feldom, lying on the edge of the Yorkshire Dales National Park and astride Swaledale – arguably one of the most beautiful parts of Britain. Here we have a positive conservation policy, formulated and developed through a Conservation Group of military and civilian experts. I commend their work to you"

H.M. Rose, Major General GOC NE District, 18th May 1990

At first glance it may seem that the requirements of environmental and archaeological conservation are incompatible with military activity. It is perhaps surprising then to realise that the preservation of this landscape is due largely to the military stewardship of the Training Area. Over time it has held in check large-scale afforestation and intensive farming, and in so doing has enabled components of the historic landscape to survive, several ecological habitats to be designated and even a nature reserve to be created! Prehistoric rock carvings, Iron Age forts, deserted medieval villages, 47 Scheduled Ancient Monuments and industrial mining remains are visible to the discerning eye...all within an area recognised for its natural beauty and diversity of flora and fauna.

At the forefront of this stewardship is the Catterick Training Area Conservation Group which hosts a variety of subject matter experts – military and civilian, amateurs and professionals alike – with a shared interest in the sustainable use of the Training Area. From its foundation in the 1970s, Conservation Group members have worked to generate a large body of research, and it is on the back of this knowledge that it has been possible to produce this book. The very existence of the Group demonstrates that military training and conservation are not mutually exclusive and should be celebrated as Catterick Garrison reaches this very important milestone it its history.

As Lieutenant Colonel Holden mentions in his foreword the production of this book has been timed to commemorate a chain of events that took place in the 20th century and which have left an indelible mark on our national identity. In 1915 Catterick Garrison was established to train troops for WWl and, as the century progressed, for WWII and other military engagements. In 2015 Catterick Garrison celebrates its centenary and it is entirely appropriate that this book is dedicated to all those who trained in Catterick Camp, but especially to those who made the ultimate sacrifice and did not return from the battlefield.

Acknowledgements

We are grateful to the following people and organisations who have encouraged and contributed to the production of this book. Lieutenant Colonel Mark Holden and Major (Retd) Tony Crease, Commander and Deputy Commander of SD Training North respectively and Graham Newcombe a Senior Estate Surveyor in the Defence Infrastructure Organisation (DIO), gave their backing throughout the course of the project. Major (Retd) Tim Helps kindly loaned the editor his earlier prototype for this production. Subject matter expertise and articles in the fields of geology, mining, archaeology and ecology have been provided by Richard Almond, Lawrence Barker, Tim Laurie and Dr Moira Owen who have all waited with admirable patience to see the results of their labour. Staff at Catterick Garrison Headquarters have been kind in allowing access to their archive and we are grateful to the former Garrison Commander, Colonel Nick Millen, for supplying a photographic collection of the early Garrison. We are indebted to Robert Shopland-Reed for sharing some of his knowledge of the estate as the Senior Estate Surveyor for some 25 years. We are obliged to Winifred Hodge for allowing us to include an example of her artwork, to Jez Kalkowski for providing several photographic images and to Clive Torrens, for generously allowing us to not only look through his extensive historical postcard collection but also to use a number throughout the book. Dave Edwards and Martin Meggs of the DIO Geospatial Services office at Catterick helped to source copy and obtain consent for some of the maps and Henry Boot PLC kindly gave consent to reproduce several images from their photographic archive.

The assistance provided by staff at Richmond Town Council, The Green Howards Regimental Museum and North Yorkshire County Record Office is also greatly appreciated and we are grateful that they have allowed photographs and maps from their archives to be included. The Ordnance Survey have been extremely helpful with regards the reproduction of old and current maps included in the book.

Former and present-day residents of the Training Area richly deserve thanks for sharing their knowledge and experiences. In particular this extends to Bob Dixon, John Joe Pettit, David and Jean Calvert, and Doris West. Their provision of historic documents, photographs and memories has been nothing short of invaluable.

Jane Hatcher and Colin Grant were kind enough to review the draft manuscript and we are grateful for their helpful comments and conversations. A large debt of gratitude is owed to Josephine Haskett of Landmarc Support Services Ltd who not only provided several images but also worked tirelessly and patiently on the manuscript and proofs in order to meet the tight publication deadline.

However, the editors take full responsibility for any errors or inaccuracies that might have crept into the text. Furthermore, any views expressed are those of the authors and do not necessarily represent those of the Department/ HM Government.

We have tried to acknowledge all the images but where this has not been possible the attribution has been left blank.

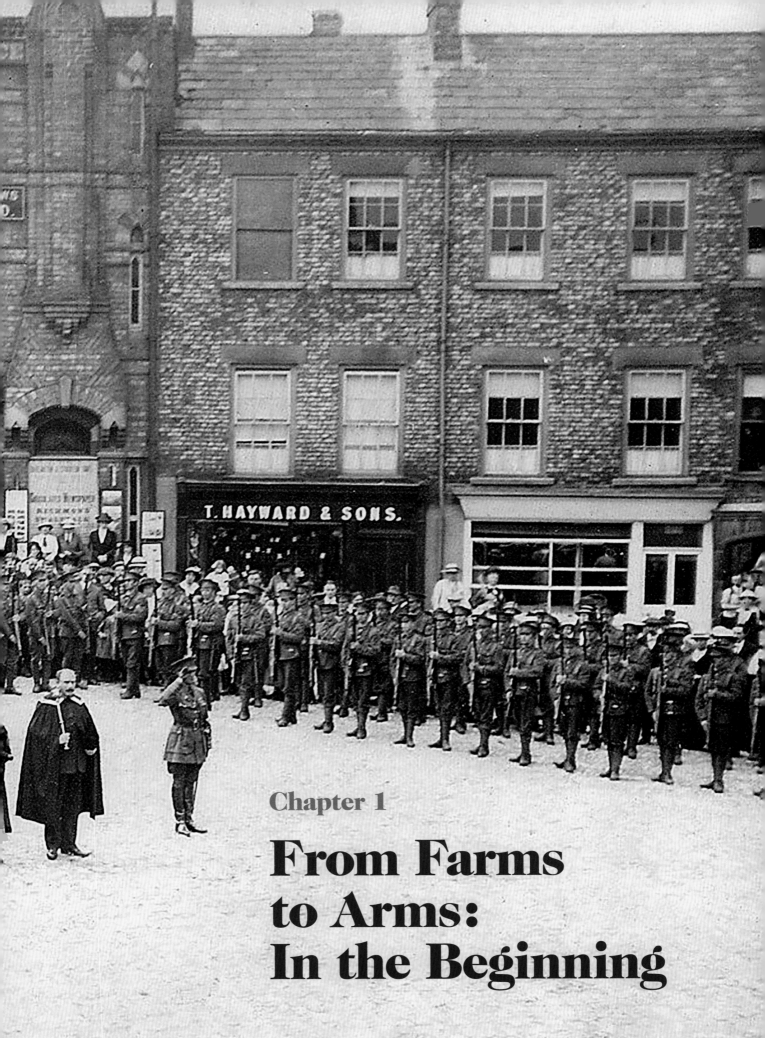

Chapter 1

From Farms to Arms: In the Beginning

From Farms to Arms: In the Beginning

Standing beside the busy roundabout at 'Camp Centre' today you may find it hard to imagine that this area was once prime farmland in the rural parishes of Hipswell and Scotton *(Figure 1)*. Today they are largely subsumed within the Garrison but at one time they were distinct entities – snug villages situated between *'the many streams that come coursing down from southern moors and sing their songs of peace by many a cottage home'* and surrounded by countryside described as *'picturesquely diversified by hill and dale.'* [1]

Figure 1: The 1st edition Ordnance Survey map of 1857 showing the Hipswell, Scotton and Colburn Estates. At this date it is primarily an agricultural area with a patchwork of fields interspersed with a few farm buildings and woodland plantations (Ref: 40YSE19NE).

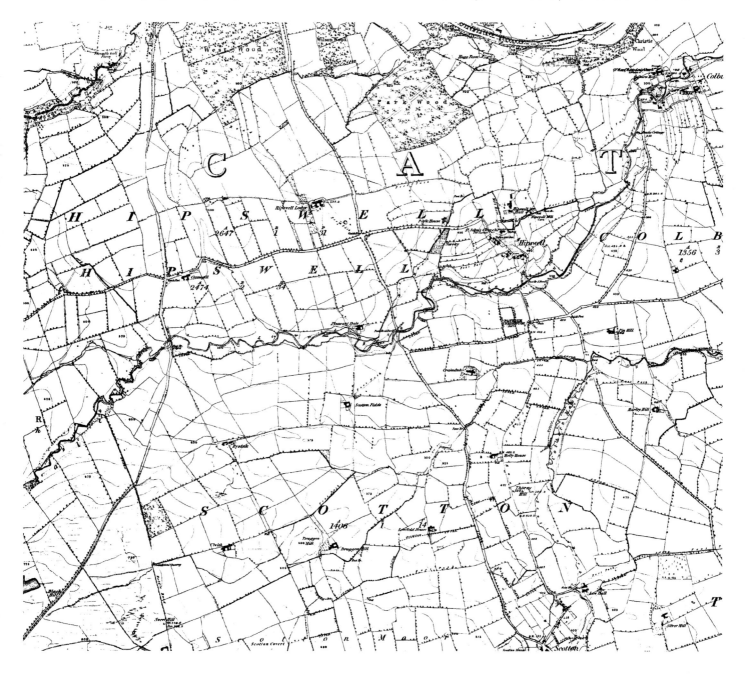

Both areas can boast a long history; Hiplewelle and Scottune, as they were called in the Domesday Book, were held by the Saxon lords Tor and Gospatric in 1066. Hipswell also merits special mention as the reputed birthplace of Oxford theologian John Wycliffe in c.1325, whose religious teachings, coupled with his production of the first English translation of the complete Bible, are thought to have paved the way for the Reformation. Radical preacher aside, these parishes could have remained in obscurity were it not for the fact that they are situated in a region all too familiar with the interest of armies throughout the ages. Nearby Catterick village, from which the Garrison takes its name, is synonymous with the Roman fort and settlement of *Cataractonium (Figure 2)*, a name that is thought to derive from the 'cataract' or falls on the nearby River Swale. The strategic military importance of this early garrison owes much to the fact that it guarded the position where the Roman Great North Road crossed the River Swale. Much later, at the close of the 18th century, the Catterick Armed Association Corps of Infantry was

formed to join a country-wide volunteer army in response to the threat posed by a revolutionary France. In 1860 there are records of the 1st North Riding of Yorkshire being deployed – with men from Hipswell, Scotton and Colburn within their ranks. And in the early 20th century, Catterick, in much the same way as hundreds of other little agricultural communities all over rural England, played its part in world events. It is somewhat poignant that near to Catterick village, just west of the original Great North Road, there now stands a simple stone plinth to mark the event which changed the face of this area forever. The inscription it bears reads:

SACRED TO THE MEMORY OF THE OFFICERS, NON-COMMISSIONED OFFICERS AND MEN OF CATTERICK CAMP AND AERODROME WHO FELL IN THE GREAT WAR 1914-18. MAY THEY REST IN PEACE.

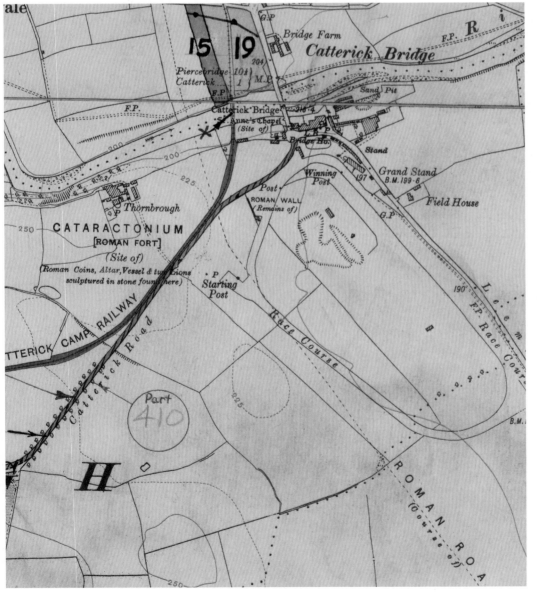

Figure 2: The site of *Cataractonium* Roman Fort. Remains of a Roman wall and the line of the Roman Road are also depicted. This is based on a 1932 Ordnance Survey map which records the area before the construction of the modern-day A1, which cuts through some of these important sites (© Crown).

1. Cole, Lieutenant Colonel Howard N., The Story of Catterick Camp, The Forces Press, Aldershot, 1972, p.6

The Making of an Army Camp

A little more than a 100 years ago, in 1908, Lord Baden-Powell, General Officer Commanding (GOC) The Northumbrian Division, was tasked by Lord Kitchener of the War Office to survey a suitable place for a new military camp in the North of England. At this time the Divisional Headquarters was based in Richmond Castle *(Figure 3)* and, after some deliberation, in 1914 a large area of open countryside around the villages of Hipswell, Scotton and Colburn was selected *(Figures 4, 5, 6, 7)*. Comprising mainly arable farmland, broken up by the occasional building or farmstead, the Camp took in the Scotton Hall Estate owned by Mrs. Stevenson, the Hipswell Estate of the Prior Wandesforde family, parts of the Colburn Estate of the D'Arcy-Hildyard family and the Brough Estate of Sir Henry Lawson.

Figure 4 (left): Before the decision was made to establish a more permanent Camp at Catterick, most accommodation would have been in tents (Catterick Garrison HQ collection).

Figure 3 (above): Richmond Castle showing the extension on the tower in which Lord Baden-Powell lived for a time (Archive Department of Richmond Town Council).

Figure 5: Declaration of War in the Market Place Richmond, 1914 (Green Howards Regimental Museum, Richmond).

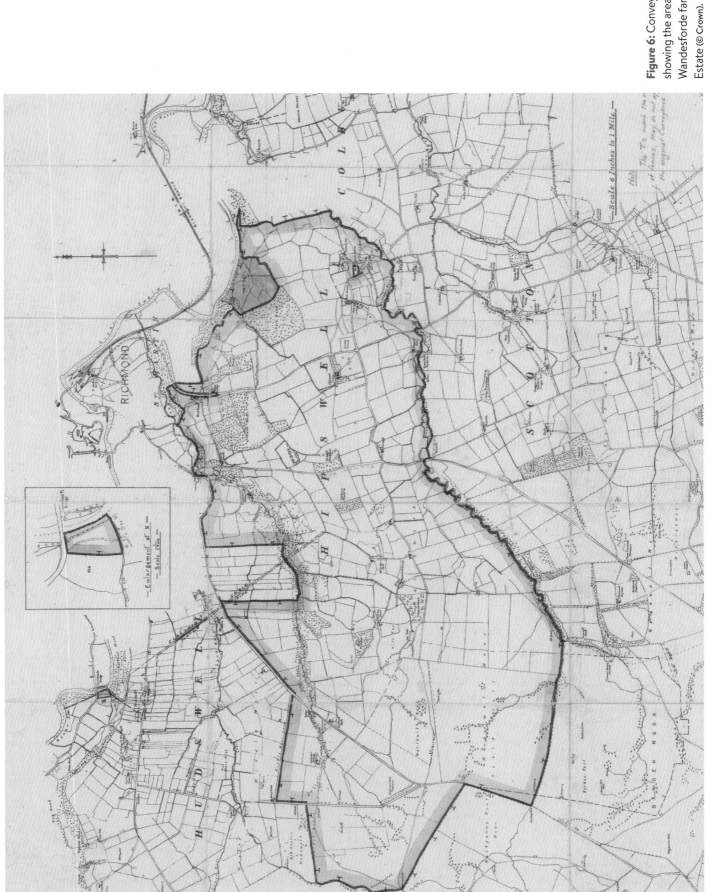

Figure 6: Conveyance map showing the areas of the Prior Wandesforde family Hipswell Estate (© Crown).

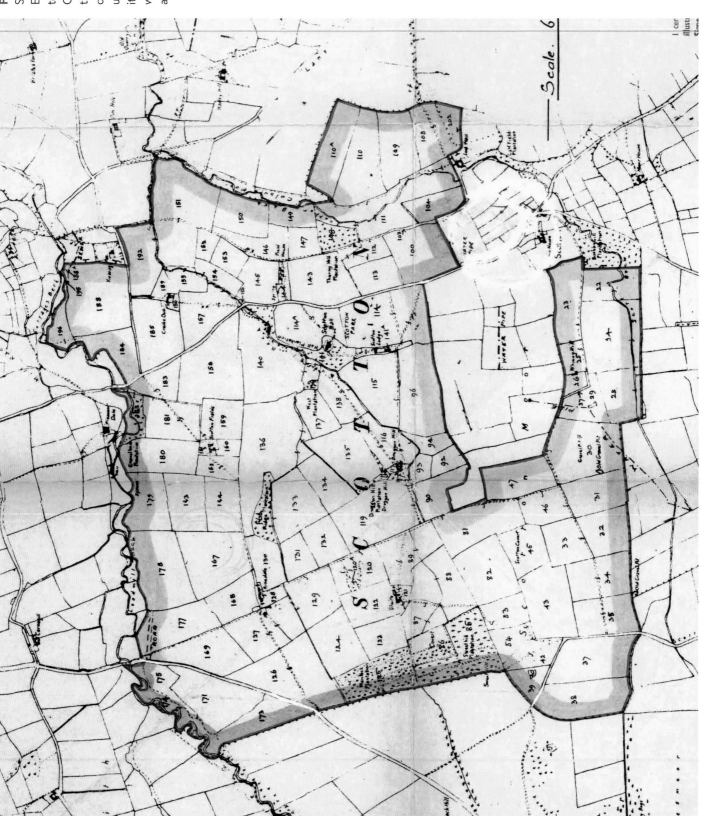

Figure 7: Area of the Stevenson family Scotton Estate that was apportioned to the first Camp at Catterick. As with Hipswell, the land was not formerly conveyed to the War Office until February 1924 once it became clear that this was to be a permanent arrangement (© Crown).

Figure 8: Hipswell at the beginning of the 20th century (Catterick Garrison HQ collection).

It is perhaps difficult to imagine just how rural this area was at the time *(Figure 8)*. It was described by Major General Sir George Scott-Moncrieff thus; *'as quiet a spot as any in England'* whilst almost reluctantly acknowledging *'the peaceful countryside soon to be invaded and disfigured by groups of unlovely huts.'* [2] Sir Henry Lawson's Agent records that in 1911, 20 pheasants were bagged by a shooting party out from Hipswell Lodge. History records where the party would have taken place but as for evidence…the site of the butt now lies beneath an Aldi supermarket, with the birds having been driven from a belt of woodland which once graced the site of the present-day Tesco!

Local opposition to the Camp's construction, in what was good sporting and agricultural land, was assuaged by the thought that it would only be a temporary wartime measure. But in all likelihood Kitchener was looking to the long term when he referred to it in 1914 as *'An Aldershot of the North.'* [3] The existence and success of the Garrison today shows just how prophetic that judgment was.

Early warnings of the changes to come were heralded by the disappearance of many old landmarks: narrow paths and lanes were widened and ancient footpaths and bridleways vanished as the ground was fast swallowed up. Work began on Richmond Camp in Spring 1915 and Sheffield-based construction firm Henry Boot was contracted for a sum of £250,000 to build a hutted camp suitable for the accommodation of some 40,000 men. The speed at which this took place seems to have taken some of the locals by surprise and there are records of carts of timber and steamrollers being driven through crops as the rapid advance of the newly-built huts encroached on their land before the harvest could be gathered.

Gangs of labourers, among them fishermen from Lowestoft and Yarmouth made unemployed by Naval operations in the North Sea, arrived to work on the site. Originally known as Richmond Camp in 1915 [4], it was renamed Catterick Camp (to avoid confusion with Richmond in Surrey!) with further designations of Catterick (Hipswell) Camp and Catterick (Scotton) Camp *(Figures 9, 10)*. The name Catterick was adopted because it was close to Catterick village and Catterick Bridge railway station which served as the main station to the camp. The military association with the former Roman fort at Catterick may have also played a part.

The huts were constructed in 'Lines' which were labelled alphabetically from A to Z. As fast as they were built they were occupied, with the first troops moving into barracks in October of 1915. The speed at which this took place meant that adequate paths and roads had not been laid between the lines of huts. Inevitably the wet and windy conditions for which Catterick is (in)famous soon created muddy quagmires, churned up by the boots of hundreds of men, wagons and horse-drawn transport, a dismal pre-taste of conditions they were soon to encounter elsewhere:

'Boots that had squelched through the Catterick mud went on to sink into the mud of Passchendaele and the Somme and the Camp was identified with the conditions which obtained during their training for war.' [5]

2. Ibid. p.13
3. Ibid. p.13
4. Hatcher, J., The History of Richmond, North Yorkshire. From Earliest Times to the Year 2000. Blackthorn Press.
5. Cole, Lieutenant Colonel Howard N., The Story of Catterick Camp, The Forces Press, Aldershot, 1972, p.25

16

Figure 9 (left): A Royal Engineers map of Catterick Camp, Scotton Division, dated 14th October 1915 (note that the name 'Richmond' Camp has been amended). Formerly a rural area, the farms and fields have now been swamped by huts. The railway infrastructure is already in place (© Crown).

Figure 10 (opposite page): A Royal Engineers map of Catterick Camp, Hipswell Division, dated 11th February 1916. A key in the top left corner helpfully records the symbols used to depict hut functions (© Crown).

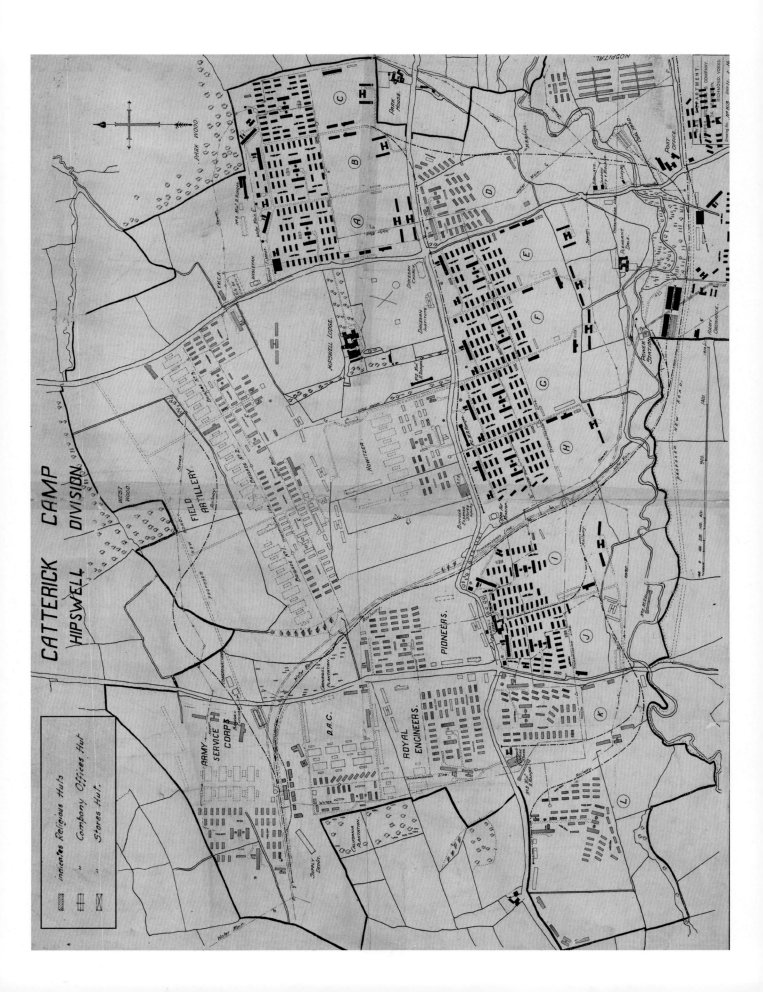

Figure 11 (left): An early picture of Rimington Avenue. The road, nowadays a continuation of the Richmond Road, connected Richmond Station to Catterick Camp. It was built in 1916 by German Prisoners of War and at the time was locally known as 'German Road' (Catterick Garrison HQ collection).

Figure 12 (below): Conveyance map for land belonging to the Prior Wandesforde family. It depicts the proposed route for Rimington Avenue (© Crown).

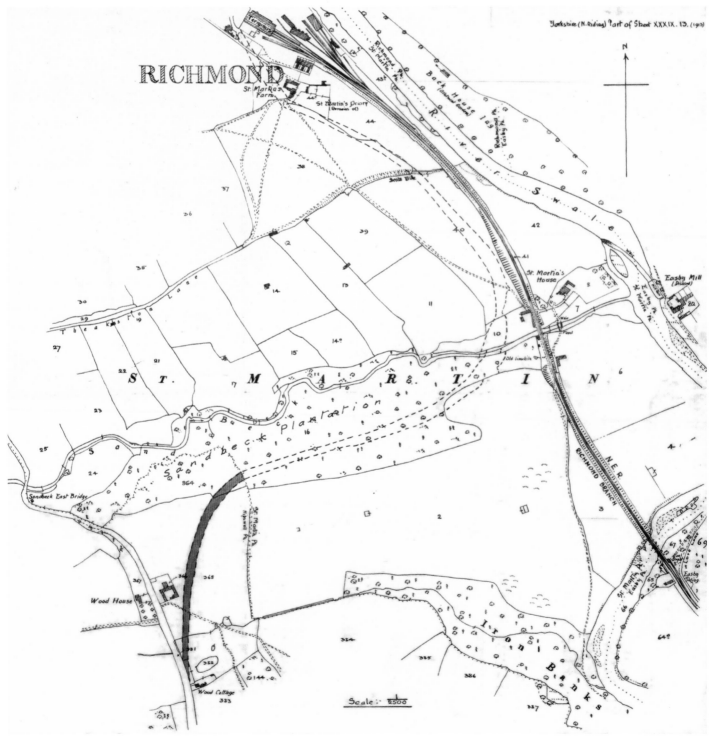

Figure 13: Catterick Bridge: The medieval road bridge was used as a temporary railway bridge (Henry Boot Archive).

Figure 15: Central Station, Catterick Camp (Catterick Garrison HQ collection).

Figure 14: Catterick Bridge: The finished new railway bridge (Henry Boot Archive).

The arrival, in 1916, of more than 5,000 German soldiers when Catterick became a Prisoner of War Camp, bolstered the infrastructure construction efforts, including the road linking Richmond Station with the Camp. The road was named Rimington Avenue after the Camp's first Commandant, Major General M.F. Rimington *(Figures 11, 12)*.

Materials for the construction of the Camp were brought in by a specially-built light railway running from Catterick Bridge, with spurs leading to the various sites and depots. The Camp had to be self-sufficient, with roads, railways, electricity, water supply and sewage works all being built from scratch. The light railway was dismantled on completion of the works leaving only the main line which ran from Catterick Bridge to near the present-day Garrison centre. This line crossed the River Swale using the medieval road bridge – constructed in the reign of Henry V in 1421 – and it was not until 1922 that this ancient bridge was superseded by a metal girder bridge to carry trains across the river *(Figures 13, 14)*. At the centre of the Camp was Central Station, located opposite the old Military Hospital on the Catterick Road. This was little more than a Halt, but from 1915 onwards it was the point where many hundreds of thousands of troops started their journey to the Western Front *(Figure 15)*.

Forgotten Facts

An Ancient marker

During the construction of Rimington Avenue a large erratic glacial rock was discovered and placed near the station beside the new road. Next to the War Office initials and date 1917-1918 it is inscribed with Latin text which translates as 'O powerful one move me if you can'.

Life on Camp during WWI

Living conditions within the huts were fairly primitive. Designed to accommodate 15 men they were often overcrowded with 30 to 40 fighting for bedspace. The only source of warmth was provided by a slow combustion stove in the centre of each hut, whilst ablutions were taken in open-sided huts fitted with zinc bowls *(Figures 16-20)*.

Figure 16: Catterick Camp huts c.1917 (Catterick Garrison HQ collection).

Figure 17: Huts being constructed in 'A' Lines, Hipswell Camp (Henry Boot Archive).

Figure 18: Construction of Army Service Corps huts at Scotton Camp (Henry Boot Archive).

Figure 19: Sewer construction between huts at Scotton Camp (Henry Boot Archive). In 1915 Richmond Council inspectors repeatedly asked for plans of the drainage and sewer arrangements at Catterick Camp. By the end of the year 'sickness with diphtheria' were reported as the Camp struggled to maintain its increasingly burdened infrastructure (Source: Richmond Council Minutes, 1912-1918. North Yorkshire County Record Office: Mic 2848).

Figure 20: Cook House and Dining Room (Henry Boot Archive).

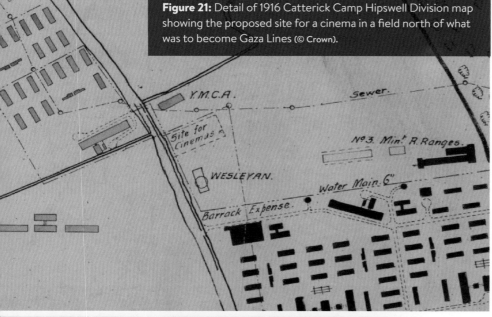

Figure 21: Detail of 1916 Catterick Camp Hipswell Division map showing the proposed site for a cinema in a field north of what was to become Gaza Lines (© Crown).

Training dominated the lives of the troops: from early morning physical training through to a daily round of bayonet fighting, bombing, musketry, route marches and all aspects of trench warfare, including night operations, moving under cover, cutting the wire and crossing No-Man's-Land to get to their objective. The hardships of life were mitigated, to some extent, by rudimentary, but increasingly imaginative, entertainment. In nearly every Lines a hut was rigged up with a crude stage for a variety of acts or regimental concert troupes. By 1918 there were four cinemas in the Camp including one that had formerly been a Darlington skating rink before being enlarged, converted and re-constructed at Harley Hill *(Figures 21, 22)*.

Perhaps most exciting was the arrival of professional showground boxer 'Professor' Bill Moore with his entourage and showground boxing booth. The booth was shaped like the quarter-deck of a battleship on which his champions would parade and strut before each show. Contests between champions, 'professionals' and all comers were on the programme, but the highlight of the evening's entertainment was when one of the Moore family would wrestle with a large bear. The show was closed by the military authorities because the bright lights and flares illuminating the booths and sideshows offered a target to Zeppelin raiders. The health and safety of bear and human alike appear not to have been a consideration.

Figure 22: This wall, situated on the Richmond Road, is the only remaining part of what was the Westwood Palace Cinema built by Thomas Pinder. The wall formed part of the steps leading up to the cinema's entrance (Jez Kalkowski, © Crown).

Becoming permanent

By 1919, after the armistice *(Figure 23)*, a sad state of affairs prevailed as thousands of bored and unoccupied troops walked aimlessly about the Camp's muddy roads. In place of the frenetic activity that had once existed, the Camp was used both as a demobilisation centre and a dumping ground for surplus stores and equipment – at one time there were over 50,000 18-pounder field artillery pieces standing in long lines, all waiting to be disposed of. Large numbers of the Camp's buildings, described as being of cold, colourless concrete, [6] became derelict and uninhabitable. It was touch-and-go whether the Camp would shrink back to make way for a resumption of the rural life some of the local residents may have wished for. But the authorities in Whitehall had other ideas. In 1924 the Government called for the establishment of a permanent camp at Catterick, marking the turning point from hutted training camp to permanent field centre *(Figures 24a, 24b, 25)*.

Life on Camp during peace and war

The news that they were to be stationed in Catterick was not greeted with enthusiasm by many regiments. Used to the relative luxury of southern barracks a soldier from the Middlesex wrote in the Regimental Journal of 1927:

'we do not, as yet, like our new station… The coal strike caused us to be put on half rations of inferior coal and the weather has been bitterly cold… Catterick mud is a near relation to that of Flanders… Sports grounds are in their infancy, whilst we feel cramped in the reconstructed huts after the spacious barracks of Aldershot.' [7]

Training conditions were not seen as much better. *"Catterick weather has kept up its reputation throughout the quarter"* commented a contributor in August the following year, *"we are still wearing our mid-winter underclothes. Under semi-arctic conditions varied by rainstorms we have now completed the annual musketry and machine gun courses on Barden Moor."* [8]

The frequent and often heavy rainstorms also contributed to the list of complaints, collapsing tents to sodden ruins within which *'swift streams'* flowed bearing *'socks, shirts and vests.'* [9]

Perhaps spurred by such complaints the Camp developed speedily. Whilst the undaunted soldiers' spirit determined that their tents were resurrected (no doubt aided by an issue of rum and singing hard [10]), additional land was purchased and the Lines were repaired and renovated. In place of alphabetical designations they were renamed after the then recent WWI epic battles *(Figure 26)*. Vimy, Somme and Gaza are familiar, but others less so. Messines Lines was originally called Ploegsteert Lines and the COs Quarters, Ploegsteert House but, it was said, the first occupant objected strongly to having to live in 'Plug Street' – so the name was changed.

6. Cole, Lieutenant Colonel Howard N., The Story of Catterick Camp, The Forces Press, Aldershot, 1972, p.24
7. Cole, Lieutenant Colonel Howard N., The Story of Catterick Camp, The Forces Press, Aldershot, 1972, p.30
8. Ibid. p.31
9. Ibid. p.33
10. Ibid. p.33

Figure 23: Armistice Day, Richmond 1920 (Green Howards Regimental Museum, Richmond).

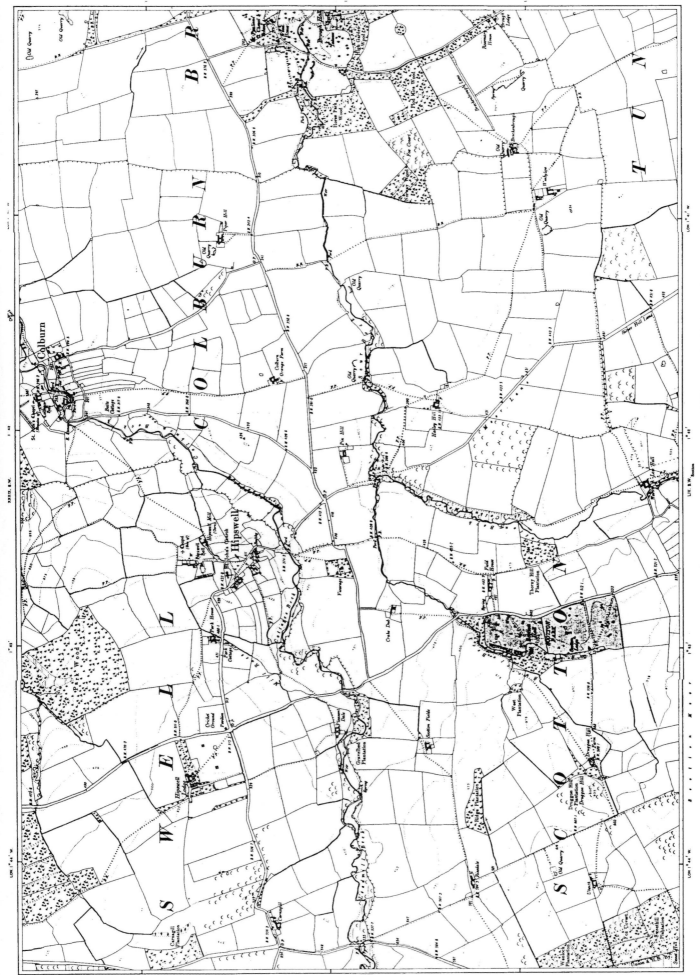

Figure 24a: 1919 edition Ordnance Survey map. The hutted Catterick Camp is not shown on this map as it was not until 1924 it was decided to make it a permanent camp.

Figure 24b: 1930 Ordnance Survey map showing the transition from a rural landscape to a built up area.

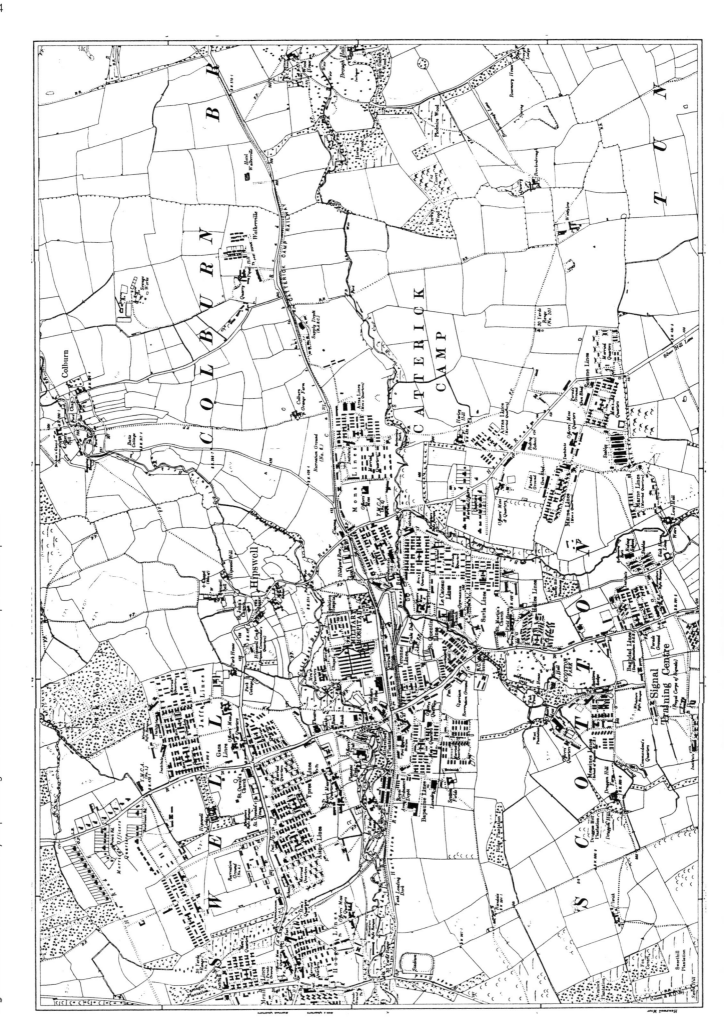

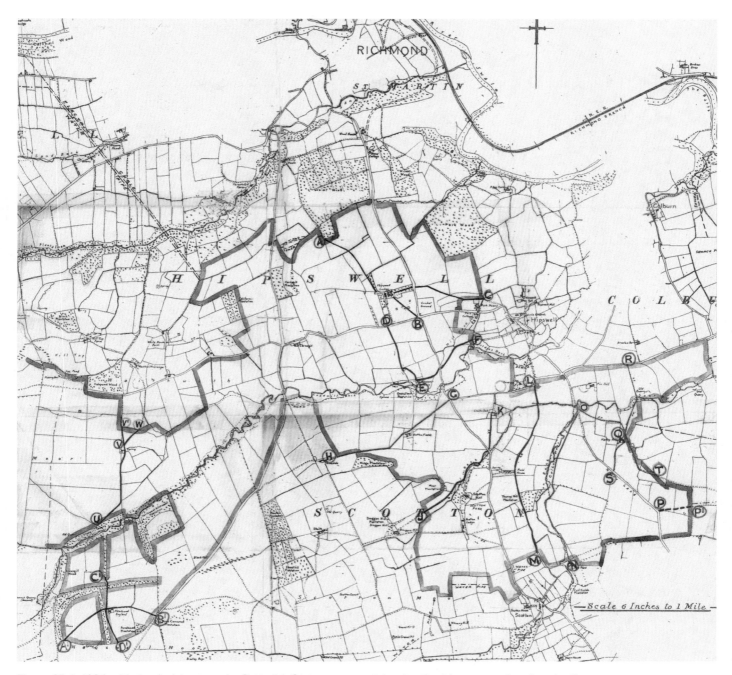

Figure 25: In 1924, with the decision to make Catterick Camp permanent, local authorities were ordered, under the Defence of the Realm Acquisitions of Land Act, 1916, to close the Rights of Way that had formerly existed within the area of Hipswell and Scotton. This area had now officially become Catterick Camp (© Crown).

Plans for married quarters were put forward. The quality of design and construction of the brick-built Officers' quarters was such that most are still in use today. Senior Officers could expect a house with three or more bedrooms with an upstairs w.c., bathroom, dressing room and servants quarters (although, rather unfairly, this would be the one bedroom without a fireplace). Soldiers' families had to make do with more basic accommodation with some being fashioned out of former barrack huts, a brick outer cavity wall concealing their former identities. Rank also dictated the amount of space allowed for

unmarried servicemen. Whilst a Field Officer was allocated a comfortable 361.6 square feet in the table of accommodation listed in a 1935 engineer's map, the 'Rank and File' soldier was granted a much trimmer 64.3 square feet (*Figure 27a, 27b and 27c*). The substantial Sandhurst Blocks, constructed in the late 1930s, may have addressed some of those inequalities. In place of single-storey barrack accommodation, were three floors accommodating up to 720 men (potentially a whole battalion), with living rooms, dining accommodation, cookhouse, offices, sitting rooms and hot water facilities (*Figure 28*).

Figure 26: 'Catterick Camp showing Roads, Principal Footpaths, Buildings & Barracks Etc'. A 1929 hand-drawn map of Catterick Camp by SQMN F. Hampson.

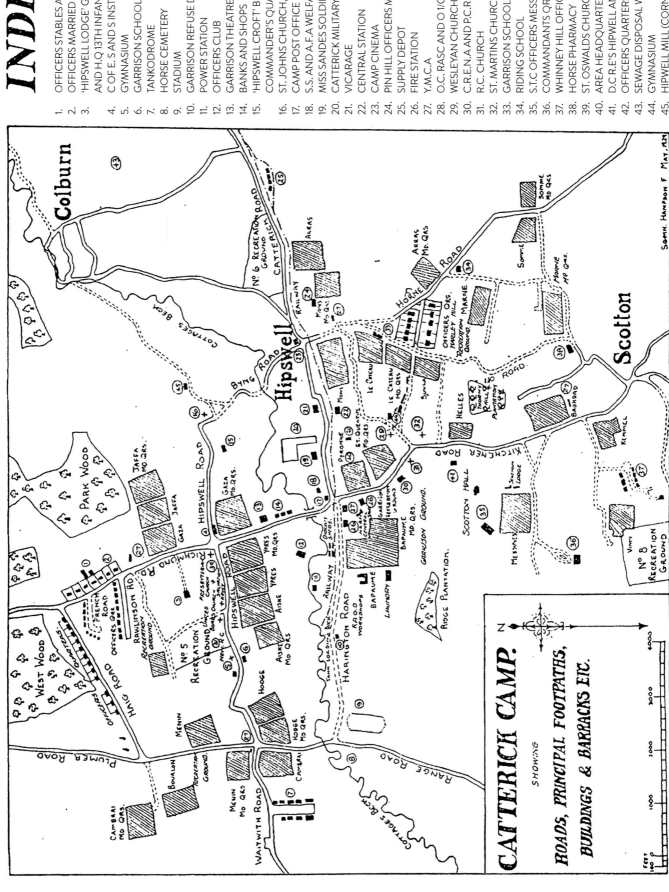

INDEX.

1. OFFICERS STABLES AND GARAGES
2. OFFICERS MARRIED QUARTERS
3. 'HIPSWELL LODGE' G.O.C. AREA RESIDENCE AND H.Q 13TH INFANTRY BRIGADE
4. C OF E. S AND S INSTITUTE
5. GYMNASIUM
6. GARRISON SCHOOL
7. TANKODROME
8. HORSE CEMETERY
9. STADIUM
10. GARRISON REFUSE DESTRUCTOR
11. POWER STATION
12. OFFICERS CLUB
13. GARRISON THEATRE
14. BANKS AND SHOPS
15. 'HIPSWELL CROFT' BRIGADE COMMANDER'S QUARTERS
16. ST. JOHNS CHURCH, & MILITARY CEMETERY
17. CAMP POST OFFICE
18. S.S. AND A.F.A WELFARE CENTRE
19. MISS SANDES SOLDIERS HOME
20. CATTERICK MILITARY HOSPITAL
21. VICARAGE
22. CENTRAL STATION
23. CAMP CINEMA
24. PIN HILL OFFICERS MESS
25. SUPPLY DEPOT
26. FIRE STATION
27. Y.M.C.A
28. O.C. RASC AND O 1/C BARRACKS
29. WESLEYAN CHURCH
30. C.R.E.N.A AND P.C.R.E (E AND M)
31. R.C. CHURCH
32. ST. MARTINS CHURCH
33. GARRISON SCHOOL
34. RIDING SCHOOL
35. S.T.C OFFICERS MESS
36. COMMANDANTS QR
37. WHINNEY HILL OFFICERS QUARTERS
38. HORSE PHARMACY
39. ST. OSWALDS CHURCH
40. AREA HEADQUARTERS
41. D.C.R.E'S HIPWELL AND SCOTTON
42. OFFICERS QUARTERS
43. SEWAGE DISPOSAL WORKS
44. GYMNASIUM
45. HIPWELL MILL (CORN)

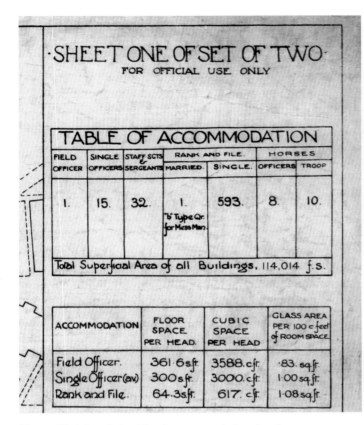

			RANK AND FILE.		HORSES	
FIELD OFFICER	SINGLE OFFICERS	STAFF SGTS & SERGEANTS	MARRIED.	SINGLE.	OFFICERS	TROOP
1.	15.	32.	1. "b" Type Qr. for Mess Man.	593.	8.	10.

Total Superficial Area of all Buildings, 114,014. f.s.

ACCOMMODATION	FLOOR SPACE PER HEAD.	CUBIC SPACE PER HEAD	GLASS AREA PER 100 c feet of ROOM SPACE.
Field Officer.	361·6 s.ft.	3588. c.ft.	·83. sq.ft.
Single Officer (av.)	300 s.ft.	3000. c.ft.	1·00 sq.ft.
Rank and File.	64·3 s.ft.	617. c.ft.	1·08 sq.ft.

Figure 27a (above): A table of accommodation showing how rank determined space allocation, taken from a 1935 Royal Engineers map of Menin Lines (© Crown).

Figure 28 (below): Sandhurst Blocks, Vimy Lines. Insets show the date on the drain hopper and the iconic clock tower of the demolished Sandhurst Block at Gaza Barracks (Catterick Garrison HQ collection).

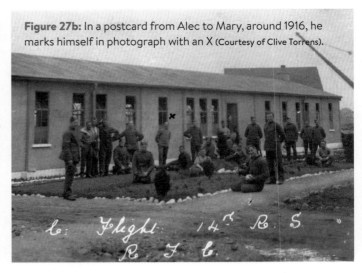

Figure 27b: In a postcard from Alec to Mary, around 1916, he marks himself in photograph with an X (Courtesy of Clive Torrens).

Figure 27c: On his second postcard, he then marks where he sleeps- as a 'Rank and File' solider (Courtesy of Clive Torrens).

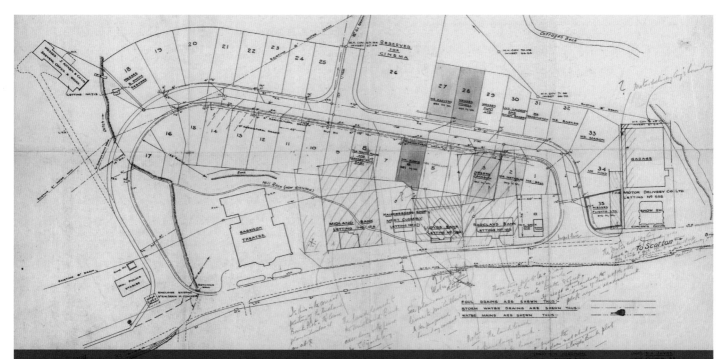

Figure 29: 1929 plan for a shopping area on Shute Road (named after Lieutenant General Sir Cameron Shute, Northern Command 1927-31). Few of the original buildings survive today; the site for the Garrison Theatre and what was the 'Ritz Cinema' (re-named Essoldo and then Classic Cinema) is clearly marked alongside sites for retail and banking outlets (© Crown).

At the same time shops and other amenities were developed and constructed *(Figure 29)*. The concrete hut which had served as the Camp Post Office since 1915 *(Figure 30)*, was replaced with a large red-brick building capable of meeting the demands of a growing population *(Figure 31)* and a series of banks, shops and cinemas were constructed on Richmond and Shute Roads *(Figures 32a, 32b, 33)*. Several NAAFI Clubs were set up offering luxury social and residential facilities for all ranks and their families. Officers meanwhile were handsomely provided for by the Officers' Club *(Figures 34, 35a, 35b)*. Built by German Prisoners of War on land formerly occupied by Pleasant Dale Farm, it opened in 1918 and boasted a bar, dining room and leisure facilities amidst plush red velvet furnishings and sporting murals. Known as a social hub in its 1930s heyday its splendour is hard to visualise, especially when looking at the Tesco complex which nowadays occupies the site; a rival certainly in numbers of visitors but not in glamour.

Belying its imposing red brick exterior the Sandes Building (now home to Command and Staff Training (North), offered a refuge and befriending service for soldiers *(Figure 36)*. Known as the Sandes Soldiers Home it opened in November 1928 and was one of many such homes established under the direction of Miss Elise Sandes CBE. Within its walls lonely soldiers could find accommodation, a library, dining and leisure facilities. One of its main features is an indoor swimming pool. Originally built as a cinema, the projection room overlooking the bath still remains.

Figure 30 and 31: The 1915 Post Office hut (Figure 30, top) was replaced in 1933 by the General Post Office building (Figure 31, bottom) (Catterick Garrison HQ collection).

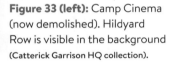

Figure 32a (top left): The original Hildyard Road, Catterick Camp, taken around 1927. Named after Mrs G. Hilyard who was distinguished for her welfare work in both WWI and WWII (Courtesy of Clive Torrens).

Figure 32b (top right): Hildyard Row, Catterick Camp following a further phase of development. Although the road is considerably more built up today the distinctive white buildings, which give the area its 'White Shops' moniker, are instantly recognisable (Catterick Garrison HQ collection).

Figure 33 (left): Camp Cinema (now demolished). Hildyard Row is visible in the background (Catterick Garrison HQ collection).

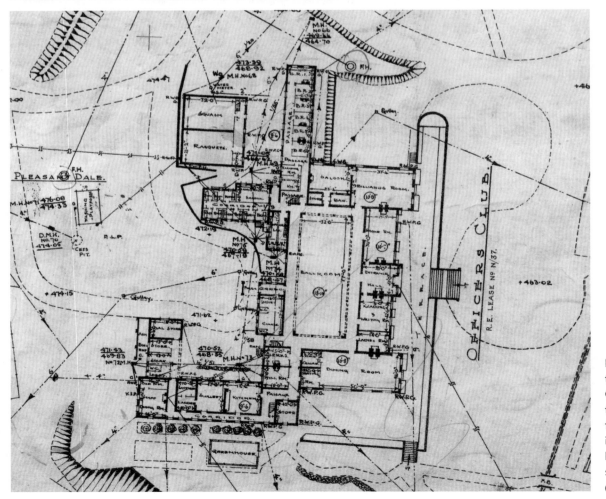

Figure 34: Plan of the Officers Club, Catterick. Built on the Pleasant Dale farmland its facilities included a ballroom, bar, games room and squash courts (© Crown).

Figure 35a (top), Figure 35b (middle): The exterior of the Officers Club, Catterick. Built by German Prisoners of War in 1918 it was demolished in the 1960s. The site is today occupied by a Tesco supermarket. Note in 35a, the original Pleasant Dale Farm is just visible to the left of the new club (Courtesy of Clive Torrens).

The needs of the sick and injured were also addressed *(Figures 37-41)*. Originally of hutted construction, the military hospital was in constant use from when it opened in 1915 and was one of the busiest in the Army Medical Services during both World Wars. In 1925 it was reconstructed and an additional 14 wards built. Its convenient location opposite the Central Station offered easy transfer of injured service personnel to a hospital bed and then, if possible, a swift return to the front line. The 1932 plan shows 48 buildings in the complex and a separate isolation block. Surrounded by a wire fence this complex housed wards for skin complaints and tuberculosis but by far the majority of buildings housed the VD wards, demonstrating the hazards of what was obviously a popular form of entertainment behind the front line! All that remains of the hospital today are the gardens and a lily pond next to the Sandes Home although, somewhat alarmingly, what is today the Headquarters of the Garrison Dental Service was once the Garrison Mortuary! Consecrated military ground was also created and the war graves of 64 WWI soldiers are situated in a peaceful corner of the Parish Church of St John in Hipswell. In 1926, in an area adjoining the churchyard, a new military cemetery, designated the Garrison Cemetery, was opened and consecrated.

Figure 36: Early photograph of the Sandes Soldiers Home, now Command and Staff Training North building (Courtesy of Clive Torrens).

Figure 37 (top left): The construction of the first military hospital at Catterick Camp (Henry Boot Archive).

Figure 38 (top right): In 1925 a new military hospital was built at Catterick Camp to replace the earlier huts (Catterick Garrison HQ collection).

Figure 39: Patients and their nurses, circa 1916-17 (Courtesy of Clive Torrens).

Figure 40: Ground floor plan of the Catterick military hospital, one of the country's busiest hospitals during WWI and WWII (© Crown).

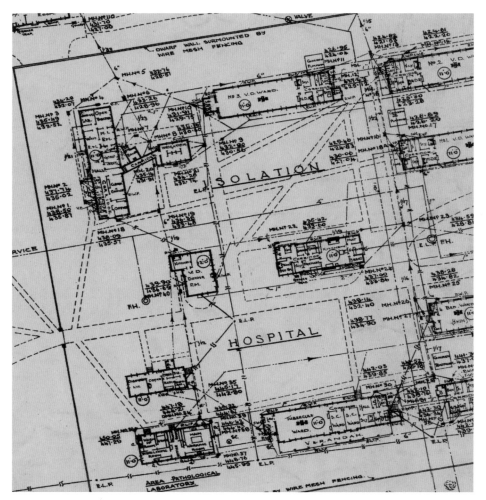

Running like a life-line throughout the Camp was the Catterick Garrison railway system *(Figures 42, 43, 44)*. During its 50 year existence [11] the railway served the needs of the soldiers, whether it was for postings,[12] leisure (at weekends several connecting services ran to London and other major cities) or to transport the sick and injured. In addition, construction materials were conveyed together with tanks and, during WWII, heavy cross-channel type guns.

11. The first junction with the national railway system was made in October 1924, the last train ran in October 1964. Source: The Catterick Garrison Gazetteer of Recorded Sites and Evolution of the Garrison 1914 to 2001, p.5, North Yorkshire & Cleveland Study Group
12. Within 10 days of receiving the order on 1 September 1939 to mobilise troops the first units were on the trains from Catterick Camp Station bound for the Southampton and Cherbourg. Source: Cole, Lieut. Colonel Howard N., The Story of Catterick Camp, The Forces Press, Aldershot, 1972, p.39

Figure 41 (above): Tasked to deal with infections such as TB and venereal diseases the Isolation Hospital's detached status and wire fence ensured contamination could not spread (Catterick Garrison HQ collection).

Figure 43: Catterick Camp railway crossing the roundabout at Camp Centre (Catterick Garrison HQ collection).

Figure 44: Train crossing at Catterick Camp Centre (Catterick Garrison HQ collection).

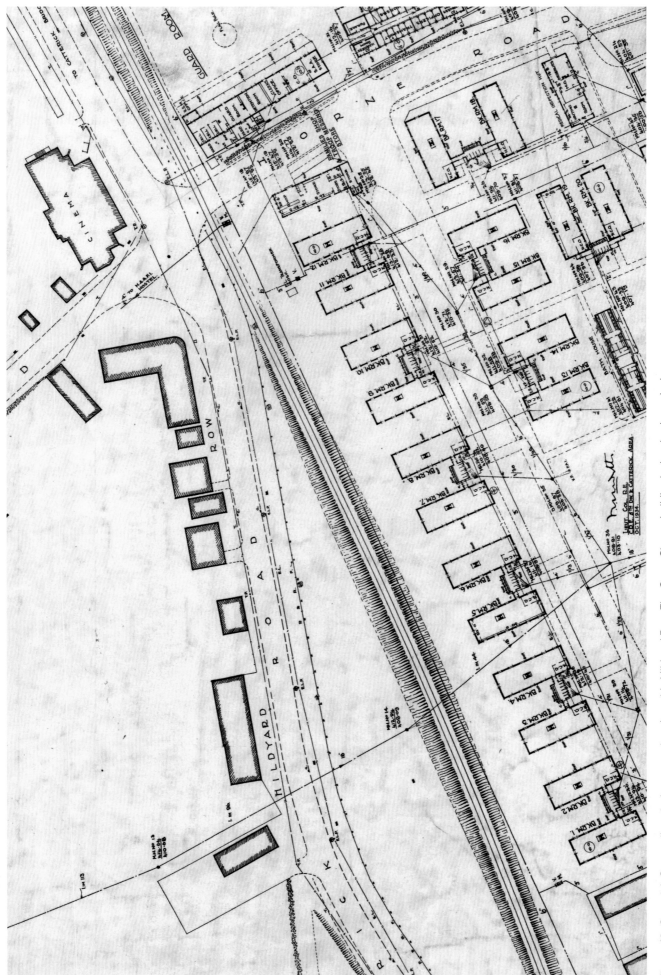

Figure 42: Catterick Camp railway is shown running alongside Hildyard Row. The Camp Cinema building is also clearly marked (Catterick Garrison HQ collection).

34

Horse Power!

With its infantry training credentials the horse has never featured greatly in memories of Catterick Camp. But despite this, a glance at the 1930s Terrier maps reveals just how all-embracing and important a role in camp life the horse played. Cartways, the predecessor of roadways, criss-crossed the Camp. Many of the Lines were adjoined by large stables, while a plethora of saddlers, wheelers, forges, shoeing sheds and farriers all played their part in supporting horse-power *(Figures 45-49)*. Accommodation lists drawn up for each Line recorded not only the different ranks of men who occupied the Lines but also the number and type of horses they would be using. Thus we learn that some beasts were chosen as 'transport horses', some were 'troop' while others were specifically designated as 'officer'.

The horses' work within the camp varied whether for transport, construction or assisting on military exercises. An account related to the building of rifle ranges on Barden Moor in WWI shows what a central role horses and mules had in Catterick Camp's early days. The author recalls that during the ranges' construction there were *'sixty men to look after a hundred and four animals, clean all the harnesses and the wagons'*. The strength of the partnership between man and beast enabled rapid, efficient construction although not all relationships ran smoothly:

'a collection of horses and mules arrived... it was very amusing to see the way those animals took to their new owners, particularly the mules; most people gave them a wide berth.' [13]

The Military Police Headquarters included a stable for up to eight horses at the rear while the Royal Corps of Signals, who at this point depended upon the horse for their work, included a centre dedicated to the well-being of horses within their Baghdad Lines site. Any horses that should fall ill or were injured could be treated at the Sick Horse Lines (with its operating theatre) or obtain medicine from the Horse Pharmacy *(Figure 50)*. If gentle exercise was needed to get them back onto their hooves then hydrotherapy was available at swimming baths conveniently located close to the riding stables.

13. Shakespear, Lieutenant Colonel, A Record of the 17th and 32nd Service Battalions Northumberland Fusiliers, 1914-1919, Northumberland Press Limited, Newcastle Upon Tyne, 1926, p.13

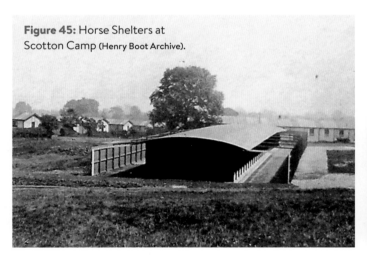

Figure 45: Horse Shelters at Scotton Camp (Henry Boot Archive).

Figure 46: Main Stable at Scotton Camp (Henry Boot Archive).

Figure 47: Picture of a Royal Corp of Signals shoeing forge at Catterick Camp (Catterick Garrison HQ collection).

Figure 48: Watering the horses at Scotton Camp 1915 (Courtesy of Clive Torrens).

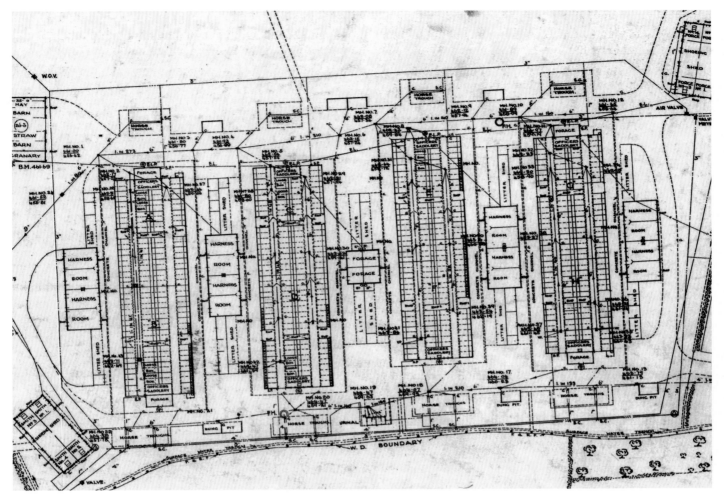

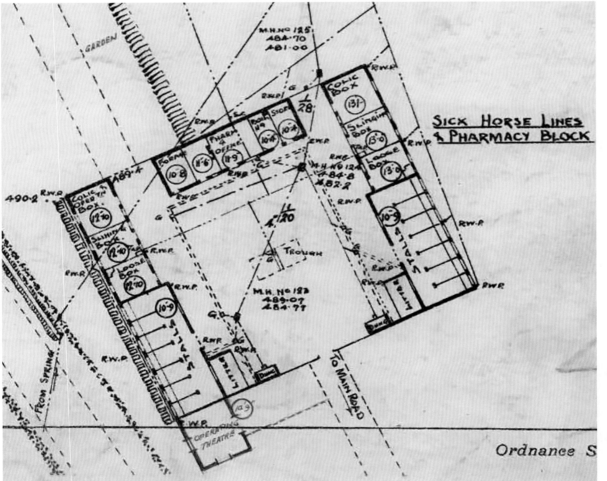

Figure 49 (above): Detail taken from 1924 map of Marne and Somme Lines showing the large stabling facilities. The stalls are surrounded by hay, straw and granary barns, several smiths, forges and shoeing sheds (© Crown).

Figure 50 (left): Detail from a plan of Bagdad Lines 1927 showing Sick Horse Lines, Pharmacy Block and Operating Theatre (© Crown).

Yet the role of the horse, however far-reaching, was relatively short-lived at Catterick Camp. The difficulties posed by a rocky moorland terrain meant that it couldn't offer the same opportunities for cavalry regiments to train as southern bases in Aldershot or Salisbury Plain. Horses, like soldiers, were susceptible to the unpredictable and sometimes severe weather conditions that prevailed at Catterick Camp. This was dramatically highlighted when a freak storm swept through the Camp in the summer of 1930 with a tragic result for the 5th Royal Inniskilling Dragoon Guards who had just returned from exercise and were preparing the evening stables:

'The sky suddenly turned a curious coffee colour. The atmosphere became oppressive; it was almost difficult to breathe. Suddenly a tremendous crash of thunder seemed to spilt the sky; a blinding flash of orange fire slashed across the gloom, and the rain teemed down – rain in stinging, bruising torrents. Out of their tents shot officers and N.C.Os, running down the horse-lines, shouting to the men to stand to their horses' heads. For the moment there was pandemonium. Terrified... the troop horses were snorting, quivering and kicking: heelpegs came up in every direction. The men got to the heads of the plunging animals and did their best to steady them. Another shattering crash and blinding sheet of light – and a trooper and the two horses he was struggling with were struck dead.' **14**

14. Ibid. p.33 Bandsman H.W. Bailey was killed on 29 August, 1930 and is buried in Hipswell Church Yard
15. Ibid. p.39

As garages began to appear alongside Officers' stables it became clear that motor power was gradually replacing horse power. Tank parks and tank sheds began to be built, the accommodation for the army's new iron work-horse. The final pin-point to the end of an era is depicted on maps which record the construction of the new tank housing area. Close by, and on land now covered by a plantation of firs, is an area simply marked 'horse cemetery'.

Throughout WWII the sole objective of Catterick Camp was to bring the war to a successful conclusion through training and preparing men for battle... an objective that was met in full. In July 1940 General Sir Ronald Adam, then GOC in C Northern Command came to Catterick and stood on high ground looking eastwards towards Middlesbrough. *"You know"* he said turning to a staff officer *"I don't think you'll ever be bombed here unless they invade – far too many interesting targets between you and the coast for the Jerries to bother with a place like Catterick."* **15** He was right and the camp was never bombed during the war *(Figure 52)*.

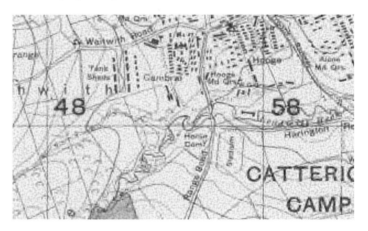

Figure 51 (above): Although blurred, the site of a Horse Cemetery is marked close to Cambrai Lines on a map of 1925. The site is now occupied by Alma Barracks (© Crown).

Figure 52 (left): 1964 postcard of Catterick Camp (Catterick Garrison HQ collection).

Far from home – POWs in Catterick Camp

Throughout its history Catterick Camp has accommodated several thousands of Prisoners of War *(Figure 53)*. In WWI Coronation Park was occupied by a large German POW compound surrounded by a high double-wire fence. Separated from their motherland and seemingly aware that they had a reputation for efficiency to live up to, the prisoners built not only roads, but also the Garrison Theatre *(Figure 54)* where they staged full-scale operas accompanied by a 60 strong orchestra (using mostly home-made instruments 'borrowed' from the ordnance store).

During WWII it was the turn of Stadium Camp to play host to another wave of prisoners. First to occupy the ground in 1942 were Italian POWs captured in the North Africa Campaigns. On their departure (when Italy became a co-belligerent nation in 1944), the camp housed Russian 'collaborators' who were taken prisoner in Normandy following the D-Day landings. Finally it was the turn of German prisoners to take up residency. Once again, proving their industrious credentials, they were organised into separate working units known as POW Companies. Within Stadium Camp two companies were housed, creating a self-contained community within the lines of Nissen huts. Gardens, rockeries and terraces were constructed along with a library, cinema and theatre. The interior decorations, paintings, murals and plaster work were described as *'masterpieces of improvisation made from scrap odds and ends. The high standard of efficiency and thoroughness characteristic of the German race'* a contemporary newspaper reporter was moved to comment *'has made a monument out of a plot of Catterick mud.'* [16]

Poignantly, Catterick Garrison has also become the final resting place for some. Within the Hipswell military cemetery a line of five Imperial War Graves Commission headstones marks the graves of Italian soldiers who died whilst POWs in 1943 and 1944. Close by, seven Polish soldiers lie buried, each of the headstones bearing the Eagle on a Shield, the national Emblem of Poland.

48471 CATTERICK CAMP, GARRISON THEATRE.

16. Ibid. p.42

Figure 53 (top): Aerial photograph of the Prisoner of War camp behind the stadium on the bend of Leyburn Road
(Courtesy of Stuart McMillan).

Figure 54 (bottom): The Garrison Theatre built by German POWs
(Catterick Garrison HQ collection).

Chapter 2

Farms Make Way for Arms: A History of the Training Area

STONE CRUSHER HERON RANGE

ELLERBY MOOR 1928.

Farms Make Way for Arms: History of the Training Area

'The early training on Hipswell and Bellerby Moors left its mark and many of the men that had driven their first tank on the Waitwith Road went into action on the Falaise Gap: many more graduated via the School of Signals to lay their lines across the desert wastes of Libya, whilst others who fired their first round on the Barden Rifle Ranges fired their last at the retreating Japanese on the Pegu-Rangoon road.'[1]

When Major General Sir George Scott-Moncrieff was ordered by General Kitchener to establish a training area between Ripon, Boroughbridge and Richmond his gaze initially alighted on Jervaulx Moor and a camp location near Thornton Steward. Alarmed at the prospect of an army camp setting up on his prized farming and hunting estate the owner of Jervaulx, Mr Moubray, advised his Estate Agent, John Maughan, to show Sir George an alternative. A site in an area known as Newfound England was chosen and the army's association with Catterick and its environs began *(Figure 1)*.

During WWI the focus of land requisition was on the Hipswell, Scotton and Colburn parishes with the adjacent moorland providing areas to practise the skills that would soon be put to use in the battlefields of France. Recent fieldwork by military historians uncovered evidence of several WWI Rifle Ranges located on Barden Moor *(Figure 2)*. These ranges had been built in 1915 presumably on the area of moorland closest to the Camp that was suitable for live firing.[2] During their fieldwork the group unearthed cartridge cases with 1915 and 1916 headstamps of the type fired by a Lee Enfield Rifle and a Lewis gun, evidence of tank ranges and a trench warfare field firing range. These would have enabled troops to practise firing at a range of targets and also train in defensive fire from the trenches. Indications on the ground of the full range layout are perhaps hard to see without an expert eye but a plan of the site on a 1930s Ordnance Survey map depicts how it would have been arranged *(Figure 3)*.

Figure 2: 'Range Construction, Bardon Moor'. A plate taken from *A Record of the 17th and 32nd Service Battalions Northumberland Fusiliers, 1914-1919*, by Lieutenant Colonel Shakespear, in 1926.

1. Cole, Lieutenant Colonel Howard N., The Story of Catterick Camp, The Forces Press, Aldershot, 1972
2. Harding, David., WWI Rifle Ranges on Barden Moor Catterick, London, 2008

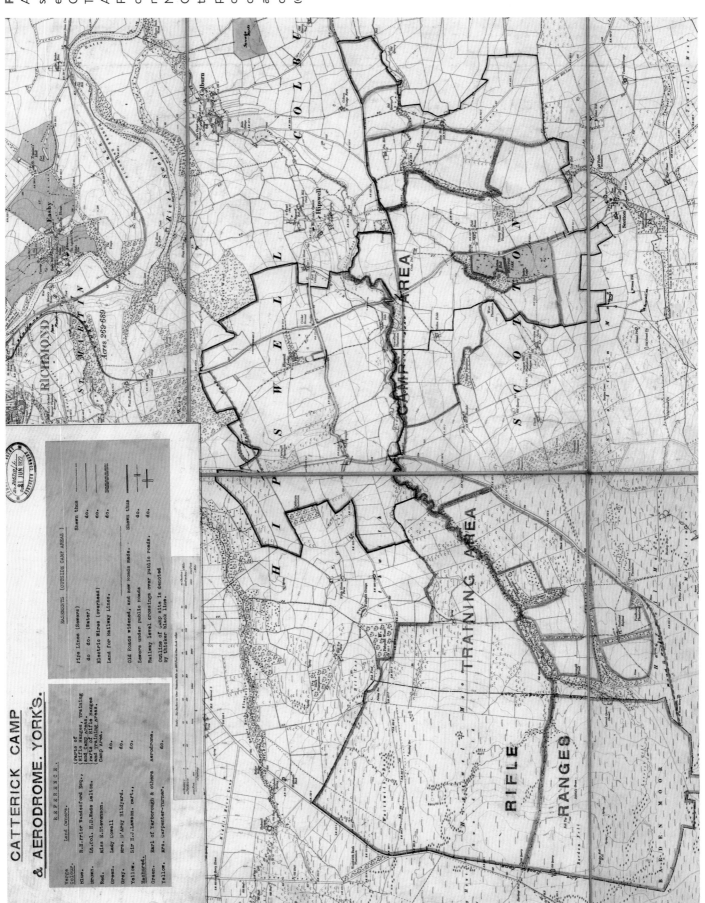

Figure 1:
A map showing the extent of Catterick Training Area in 1922. Formed out of purchases made by Northern Command, the lands' previous owners are colour-coded and marked on the legend (© Crown).

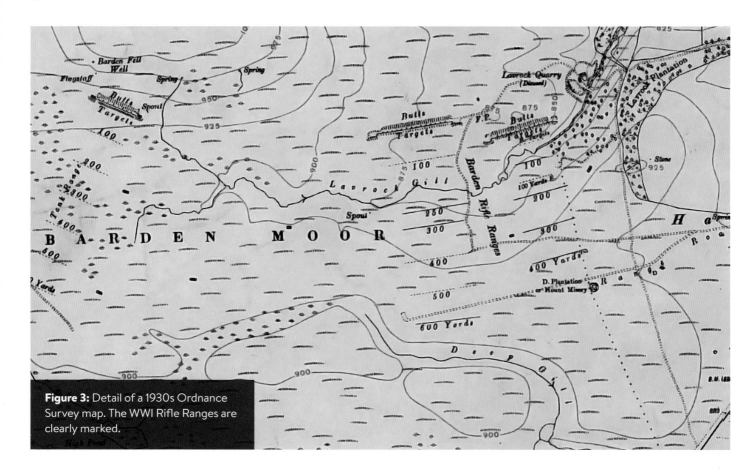

Figure 3: Detail of a 1930s Ordnance Survey map. The WWI Rifle Ranges are clearly marked.

An account was published in 1926 recalling the wartime activities of the Northumberland Fusiliers on Barden Moor. Their involvement in the range construction gives a good idea of the incredible manpower it required. Without mechanical aid a team of men, horses and mules managed to create a huge embankment, using ten to fifteen thousand tons of excavated earth, to go behind 56 duplicate targets with a four to five yard-wide trench in front:

'The rapidity with which this range was completed is said to have constituted a record… only sixteen working days were occupied, and the range was in use exactly three weeks after the first pick had been struck into the ground.'[3]

3. Shakespear, Lieutenant Colonel, A Record of the 17th and 32nd Service Battalions Northumberland Fusiliers, 1914-1919, Northumberland Press Limited, Newcastle Upon Tyne, 1926, p.13

The Training Area in WWII

By the late 1920s it was recognised that Catterick was to become a permanent garrison and not the temporary Camp some had hoped for. Initially Northern Command had attempted to appease landowners and farmers with compensation payments for the damage caused to roads, crops and the disturbance to their livestock caused by military activities. Faced with increasing pressure to find a better option than training on private land an alternative solution was found. The army would simply buy its own training areas, regardless of the cost.

To begin with Gandale (in Scotton Parish) and Barden Moor were purchased. Both these areas had been requisitioned in the Camp's earlier history but were then purchased between 1924 and 1926, an area amounting up to 7,500 acres. The following year a further 6,500 acres were added to the army's property

portfolio. Downholme Moor, Walburn and Stainton were purchased, together with their manor houses, cottages and farmsteads, and in 1928 a parcel of land at Bellerby was acquired to house the Brigade Musketry Camp *(Figures 4-7)*. Battalion camps were subsequently built in the 1930s at Wathgill and Gandale. By 1932 the War Office was in a position to produce the first map of the Catterick Training Area. The Training Area boundary shown on the map remains largely unchanged up to the present day *(Figure 8)*.

The impetus to expand landholdings followed mobilisation orders issued on 1st September 1939. As in WWI, the Headquarters at Catterick Camp were tasked with the responsibility of training young soldiers and units for battle. To fulfil this role more training ground was required and between 1940 and 1943 land which had previously formed part of the Estates belonging to the Marquess of Zetland and the Hutton family of Marske, was acquired. This area, known as Feldom

Figure 4 (right): 'Stone Crusher, Heron Range, Bellerby Moor, 1928'. Cameronian and Royal Engineer soldiers pause from their construction work to pose for the camera (Courtesy of Tim Helps).

Figure 5 (left): The original Bellerby Moor Camp, behind Deerpark Cottage 1928 (Courtesy of Clive Torrens).

Figure 6 (below): Royal Engineers at work constructing Bellerby Camp, c.1928 (Courtesy of Tim Helps).

Figure 7 (below): The Battalion on the move 'B boy leading' Bellerby Camp August 1934 (Courtesy of Clive Torrens).

Training Area, comprised more than 6,000 acres and was used extensively by both the Garrison at Catterick and the newly-formed Garrison at Barnard Castle in WWII. Additional ranges were also set up on requisitioned land near to Barnard Castle which became known as Battle Hill Ranges. From here troops practised with small arms, grenades, rocket launchers and even 25-pounders which were used to shell distant targets on the Pennines.

44

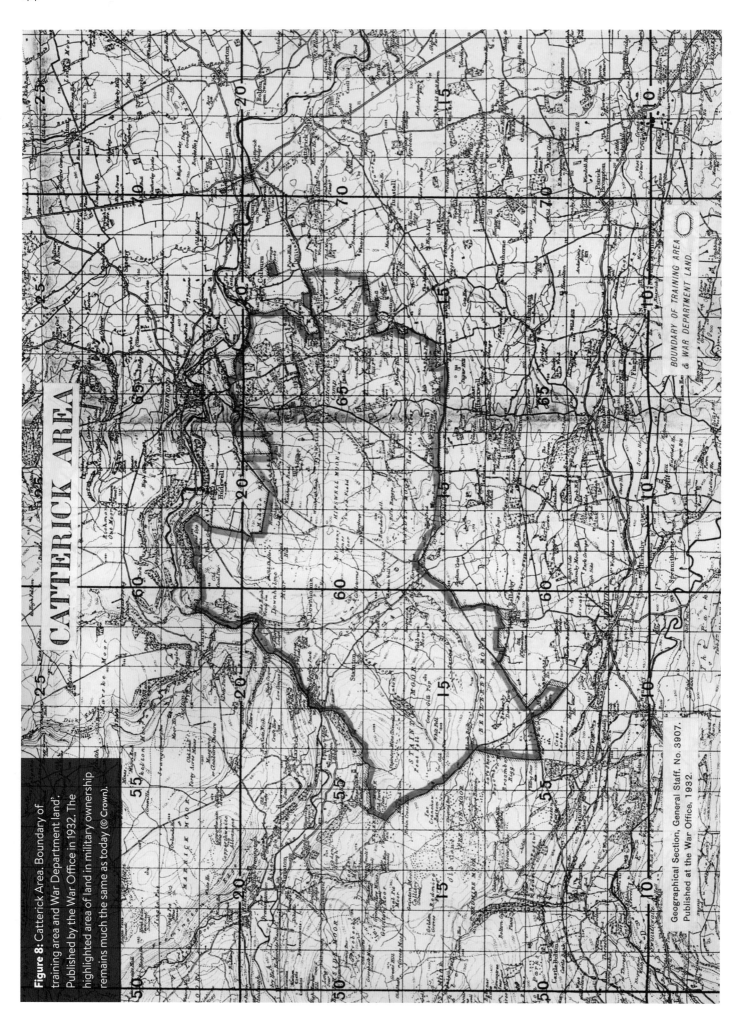

Figure 8: Catterick Area. Boundary of training area and War Department land'. Published by the War Office in 1932. The highlighted area of land in military ownership remains much the same as today. (© Crown).

CATTERICK AREA

BOUNDARY OF TRAINING AREA
& WAR DEPARTMENT LAND.

Geographical Section, General Staff. No. 3907.
Published at the War Office, 1932.

The arrival of mechanisation

Mechanisation came slowly to Catterick Training Area. Whilst horses featured large in the list of the Camp's occupants, prior to WWII military battle exercises involving cavalry were restricted to the seizing of Barden Fell with a horse-powered cavalry charge. The reluctance to use horse-power in training exercises can possibly be attributed to the terrain, an assertion borne out by comments made by a General in the 5th Inniskilling Dragoon Guards when describing training conditions in 1930:

'The training area at Catterick Camp was not particularly suitable for cavalry. Much broken up by patches of deep bog or rocky slopes, the whole area could be traversed in the course of a morning's work. In roughly the middle of the area lay some steeply rising ground, Barden Fell, which inevitably became the ultimate objective of every exercise, however framed.'

However, he concedes, it did have its compensations:

'Unrealistic as much of the training was, it was a pleasant change to get away from the roads and enclosed country around York…and to indulge of the old cavalry custom of 'galloping up the hills and riding down the umpires.'[4]

But during the course of WWII horses gave way to tanks which gradually became an increasingly familiar sight (and sound). Cavalry regiments returning to Catterick after the war all sought to continue their training using tanks and a Royal Armoured Corps Training Regiment was established. As if determined to prove that she was not entirely conquered, Downholme Moor has the distinction of claiming a tank belonging to 4 Royal Tank Regiment. It got stuck on boggy ground and sank, never to be seen again!

Folklore and myths of the Training Area

In the thousands of years that the land has supported human habitation a number of myths and folklore tales have accumulated. Names of places or landscape features often refer to a past event, person or animal and reflect the thoughts, actions and interpretations of past communities (*Figure 9*). The name 'Downholme' meaning 'in the hills' directly relates to its position at the opening of the hills, considered by early travellers as one of the entranceways into Swaledale.[5] Stainton or 'Stone-town' could refer to the fact that 'grey flags and slates' were once quarried there.[6] The Alder or 'eller' tree once grew so abundantly at Ellerton as to have impressed its name on the 'ton' or farmstead of the Saxon owners.[7] By contrast Feldom is derived from the old English meaning 'open country without trees or buildings.'[8]

Figure 9: Ancient carved stone head embedded on an exterior wall of Downholme Church. Probably Celtic, it was carved as a cult or ritual object and pre-dates the arrival of Christianity (Phil Abramson, © Crown).

4.   Evans, Major General Roger., 'The Story of the Fifth Royal Inniskilling Dragoon Guards (1951) in Cole, Lieut. Colonel Howard N., The Story of Catterick Camp, The Forces Press, Aldershot, 1972, p.33
5.   Fleming, A., Swaledale. Valley of the Wild River, Edinburgh University Press, 1998, p.8
6.   'Downholme Parish', Bulmer's History and Directory of North Yorkshire, 1890, p.421
7.   Ibid.
8.   Gelling, M., Place names in the Landscape, JM Dent Limited, London, 1984, p.236
9.   Whelan, Edna., 'Report on the visit to the site of Hartleap Well', prepared in advance of the 1988 project led by Catterick & Feldom Conservation Group to restore the site of the Well.

The hilltop spring 'Hartleap Well' which is located on Barden Fell, found fame after the poet William Wordsworth immortalised it in his 1800 poem 'Hart Leap Well'. The tale goes that a beautiful hart of legendary stamina had endured a lengthy chase across the moors in which the pursuing horses and hounds had dropped out until only a single horseman remained. Worn out at last the exhausted animal gave three tremendous leaps before dropping dead besides the Well [9] *(Figures 10, 11)*.

The final resting spot of hundreds of horses can also allegedly be found up on the lonely heights of the Feldom Moor ranges. The plantation, now marked on the map as 'Valley of Death Plantation' *(Figure 12)*, was so called after the bones of hundreds of horses were discovered during routine drainage work. The sad conclusion must be that

this is the site where many horses were shot in the economic depression that followed WWI, when it was no longer possible to feed and maintain them. In some cases there is no immediate explanation of a name – leaving its meaning open to interpretation. The topographic feature called 'Mount Misery' on Barden Moor had received its name long before the nearby WWI rifle ranges were constructed but it is quite easy to imagine soldiers training in the muddy trenches, exhausted and cold, and reflecting on how closely the Mount's name described their condition. Nearby is a point known as 'Dobbin's Grave' which perhaps, as Cole suggests, refers to an occasion *'years ago, when some faithful and favourite farmhorse was buried on the moors where he worked.'*[10] Equally mysterious are the reasons for choosing a particular site. In celebration of the Millennium a modern-day stone circle or 'mini – Stonehenge' was commissioned

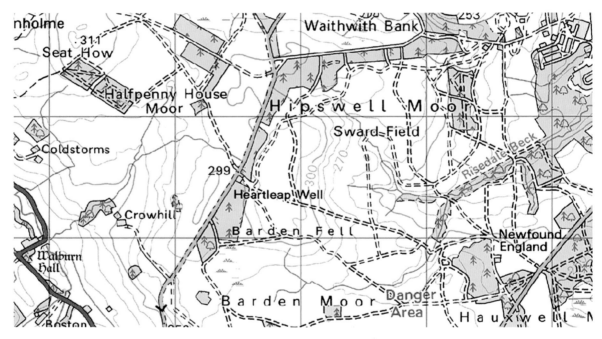

Figure 10: The site of Hartleap Well marked on a modern Ordnance Survey map (© Ordnance Survey).

Figure 11: Hartleap Well today. Perhaps not quite as Wordsworth saw it! (Phil Abramson, © Crown).

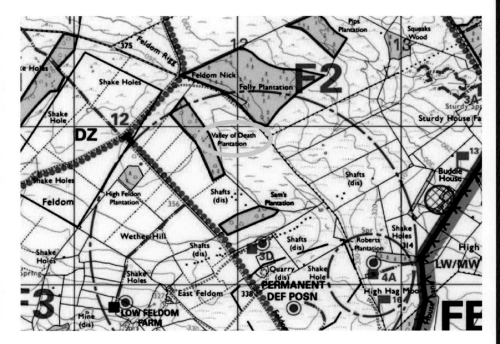

Figure 12: Site of 'Valley of Death Plantation', depicted on a Feldom Training Area map (© Ordnance Survey).

and unveiled in the small park close to Garrison Headquarters just off Scotton Road *(Figure 13)*. In a curious coincidence archaeological investigations have revealed that several thousand years ago there was once a Neolithic 'cursus' or ceremonial site located at Scorton [11] – a village close to Catterick. Curious coincidence or proof that even in our increasingly sanitised modern society the landscape still has an unspoken way to communicate!

Could the origin of some of the more unusual names be, as Arthur Raistrick suggests, simply a case of misinterpreting the northern dialect? Raistrick explains that as the original Ordnance Survey had been carried out by the largely southern-based Royal Ordnance Corps, they may have struggled to understand a Yorkshire accent:

'we must picture the soldiers of southern origin… collecting the local names from the natives there would have been much puzzling at the sound of the dialect, and many attempts to find an English word that looked something like what the local name had sounded.' [12]

Figure 13: Modern-day stone circle created to commemorate the Millennium (Jez Kalkowski, © Crown).

10. Cole, Lieutenant Colonel Howard N., The Story of Catterick Camp, The Forces Press, Aldershot, 1972, p.86
11. Fleming, A., Swaledale. Valley of the Wild River, Edinburgh University Press, 1998, p.119
12. Raistrick, Arthur., Green Roads in the Mid Pennines, Redwood Burn Ltd, 2nd Ed., Trowbridge & Esher, 1978, p.26

Figure 14: Joseph Mallord William Turner, 'Richmond, Yorkshire, c. 1819. The view from the west, looking over the plains of Yorkshire towards the Hambledon Hills' (Courtesy of Tim Helps).

Tenant farmers and the Training Area

'The 14th Infantry Brigade… were opposed by the Northland [13] troops and were ordered to try and capture Marske Bridge. The first contact was between Scotton and Gandale, and by means of quick attacks the Highlanders succeeded in getting on the line from Richmond Road to Halfpenny House just before midnight. A further night attack took part at 3.30 a.m. and they captured Seat How, Downholme and How Hill. By this time the bridge was ready for demolition by the Northland Troops. They withdrew across it and the bridge was blown up about 4.30 a.m.' [14]

The large numbers of men, horses and later, tanks, invading what had once been peaceful farmland sometimes made life extremely difficult for those who lived in, and farmed, the area.

Couple this with dramatic, loud, night-firing exercises (such as the one described above), and the tendency to destroy walls and structures, either by blowing them up or driving over them with a tank, and even the most understanding of tenants would have their patience sorely tested.

The Dixon family have farmed the land around Halfpenny House from the early 1900s and older members of the family recalled shelling and gunfire overhead as troops fired from gun battery positions on Halfpenny House Moor over to Stainton Moor. Nor were they immune from the grisly evidence hazardous training might present. At one point a makeshift mortuary was set up in one of their barns, the double-door entrance providing easy access and turning room for stretchers bearing up to 45 bodies.

Livestock were also at risk from training activities. Communication technology on exercises demanded that wires had to be laid, criss-crossing stretches of land on which sheep and cattle grazed. Downholme farmers came to dread the sight of horse-drawn carts (and latterly, specially

13. A mythical state made up for training exercises in the 1930s
14. Catterick Camp Journal, Vol. IX' (1937) in Cole, Lieutenant Colonel Howard N., The Story of Catterick Camp, The Forces Press, Aldershot, 1972, p. 36

Tel. No. : York 3031. Extension 27.
York 6262/3. (Direct Line).

Any reply to this letter should
be addressed to
THE COMMAND LAND AGENT
and the following number quoted :

LANDS/2/5912/HVP.

LANDS BRANCH,
HEADQUARTERS, NORTHERN COMMAND,
MIDDLETHORPE LODGE,
DRINGHOUSES,
YORK, YORKS.

1st September, 1942.

Dear Sir,   D.R.L.S./POST.

Ploughing-out, Catterick Camp.

Reference our recent conversation.

I have to inform you that there are no
military objections to part fields 92, 93 and
102 being ploughed-out.   I have to-day
written to the W.A.E.C. informing them of this.

Yours faithfully,

H. v. Pottayl

Command Land Agent,
Northern Command.

J.R.W. Calvert, Esq.,
Downholme Manor,
Downholme,
Richmond,
YORKS.

HVP/NJ.

Figure 15 (above): Royal Signals cable wagons carrying the spools of wire laid for communication across the Training Area (From Cole, Lieutenant Colonel Howard N., The Story of Catterick Camp).

Figure 16 (left): Letter received by J. Calvert granting him permission to plough his fields. Tenants were obliged to respect the right that the military had priority over land usage (Courtesy of Mr & Mrs D. Calvert).

adapted Land Rovers) bearing huge spools of wire waiting to be uncoiled (*Figure 15*). Experience had taught them that at least some of their sheep would get entangled once the wire was on the ground, resulting in severe injury and sometimes death.

Used to the possibly more laissez-faire tenancy that Lord Bolton's administration had offered, farmers at Downholme found the War Department a considerably less flexible landlord. Applications to graze sheep or plough a field had to be sought from Northern Command and were only agreed if the military did not need to use the land for an exercise (*Figure 16*). Understandable annoyance was felt when troops and vehicles streamed down into Downholme village from the moor above, driving straight through some stone walling that had previously served as a stock enclosure.

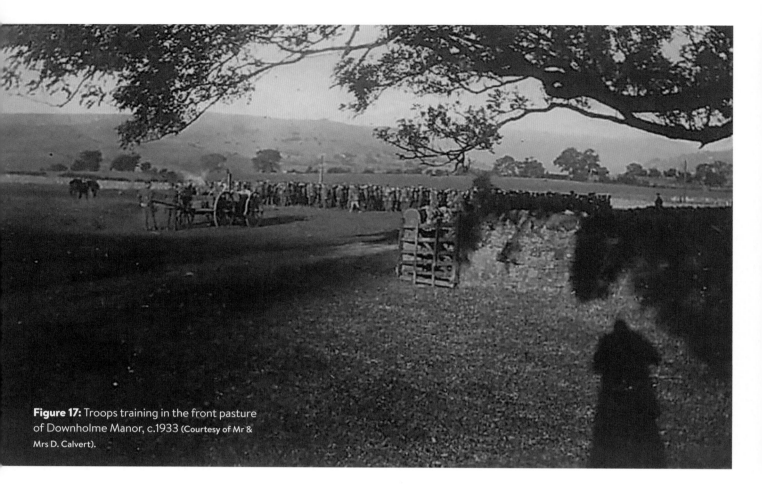

Figure 17: Troops training in the front pasture of Downholme Manor, c.1933 (Courtesy of Mr & Mrs D. Calvert).

Nor were bracken bales able to put up any form of defence when soldiers invaded the fields in which they stood. Farmer David Calvert, whose family's association with Downholme spans several generations, recollected the irritation his father felt when witnessing carefully rolled bales of dried bracken being thrown down the hill prior to the start of an exercise. *"These were bales which we used for bedding"* he described *"when they were thrown down the hill it caused them to unroll which was such a wasted effort."* The final insult came when the bales, which were of a huge size and had gathered considerable momentum on their journey down, smashed through any fences or walls in their path [15] *(Figure 17)*. Similar frustration was felt by farmers on Feldom Training Area when witnessing training exercises involving armoured vehicles and live fire. Large swathes of ancient stone walling were destroyed when narrow lanes, built for horse and cart, were forced to accommodate tanks – mechanical beasts that were much

wider and less subtle in avoiding any impediment to their path.

The realities of being within an army training area taught farmers to be vigilant in their stewardship of the land. They were quick to spot a smashed wall or open gate and the army's proclivity to stage exercises involving digging could result in the indignity of falling down a newly-dug hole. Night exercises, with the accompanying sound of explosions and gunfire, also proved trying. Any sense of satisfaction at having survived and accomplished the trials of getting children to bed was shattered by a "loud boom" echoing across the valley. [16] Even ground which at first glance did not appear obviously damaged may have had a treacherous story to tell. For instance, land that had been rented on Lord Bolton's Moor during WWII was finally handed back in 1972. Any gratitude at its return may have been short-lived with the realisation that it, and the adjoining area on Bellerby Moor,

had been targeted by thousands of 25-pounder shells fired from gun battery positions on Halfpenny House Moor during the war.

The harsh realities and necessities of war account for decisions that would otherwise have seemed heartless. During WWII when Battle Hill was requisitioned as a Training Area, it is rumoured that the farming families of East and West Loups farmsteads were ordered to evict their homes on Christmas Eve 1940. It is said that the authorities conceded to a request to allow the families to spend Christmas Day at their homes but the powers that be were unwavering in their order to evict them the day after. They were never to return *(Figure 18)*.

All credit must therefore go to the tenant farmers who have lived, and are currently living, on Catterick Training Area. Who, from first encountering the army, seem to have accepted their lot and, at points, even embraced it. Prisoners of War are remembered for helping farmers at harvest time, even bringing hand-made wooden toys much to the delight of Downholme village children. Smashed stone-walling on Barden Moor was cheerfully repaired by Italian prisoners. Nowadays the sound of instructions being shouted on Stainton Moor ranges provides Halfpenny House farmer Bob Dixon with a warning that wet weather is on the way, the rainfall being borne by the same westerly wind that carries the sergeant's voice. Livestock that have lived continuously on Training Area land have grown used to military activities and the Dixon sheep would appear to regard the sound of gunfire as almost prosaic.

Far from being antagonistic, the relationship between the army and the farmers who work the Training Area seems to be a reciprocal one. Long-established farming families have not only retained, but expanded their holdings. The extensive Training Area provides ample acreage for controlled livestock grazing which in turn helps land management. Just as the manorial holdings of old were united in the service of a powerful landlord, the network of farming families has taken pride in their role as stewards of the Defence Estate.

15. Interview with David and Jean Calvert, 7 December 2012
16. Ibid

Forgotten Facts

Tenants and the Military: a historic arrangement

Long before its ownership by the MOD, Catterick Training Area and its surroundings had known other great and powerful landlords! Almost 2,000 years ago Catterick, or *Cataractonium* as it was then called, supplied leather hides to the Roman garrison stationed in the fort of *Vindolanda*. It also provided accommodation for travellers on the route from York northwards to *Vindolanda*. We know this to be the case because Catterick is mentioned on some 1,900 year-old writing tablets excavated at the Roman fort of *Vindolanda* in Northumberland close to Hadrian's Wall. These remarkable and extremely fragile tablets date to the first century AD and provide a unique insight to life on a frontier fort in Roman Britain.

Fast forward a thousand years to a time shortly after the Norman Conquest and the resources of the land were united in the service of another military power. Based within Richmond Castle, just as Baden-Powell would be several hundred years later, Alan Rufus of Brittany relied upon the support of the subordinate lordships within his Richmondshire domain to act as a bulwark against the Scots.

Fortunately, unlike their counterparts from the Middle Ages, no defensive role is required from today's tenants, but otherwise the land could be seen to have partially reverted to its original purpose of almost two thousand years ago – supplying goods and services to a military garrison.

Figure 18: The ruins of West Loups Farm on the Battle Hill Range, County Durham (Anthony Maude, Landmarc Support Services Ltd).

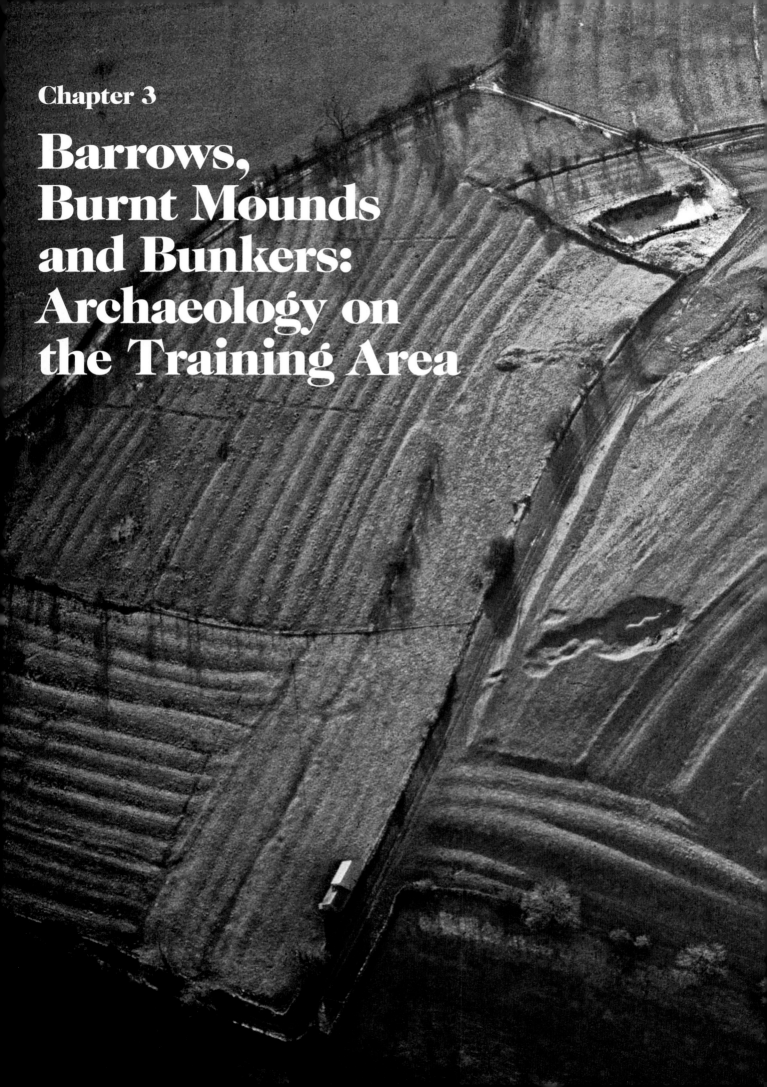

Chapter 3
Barrows, Burnt Mounds and Bunkers: Archaeology on the Training Area

Barrows, Burnt Mounds and Bunkers: Archaeology on the Training Area

The army has provided military training on the Catterick and Feldom Training Area for the best part of 100 years. Live firing, heavy vehicle manoeuvres and digging-in are all part of the training offered to army recruits, past and present. This being the case, it is perhaps optimistic to expect that fragile archaeological remains can survive on a military training area. But within this military landscape are well-preserved features of historic and archaeological interest which date from early prehistoric times to the industrial revolution. A hidden history has been woven into the fabric of the rugged moors and valleys of the Yorkshire Dales – a history that becomes visible to those who know where to look. Phil Abramson, an archaeologist who works in the MOD Conservation Section and Tim Laurie of the Catterick Conservation Group have selected several sites from the archives of the Conservation Group as representative of human activity across the Training Area from the Neolithic to the present day *(Figure 1)*.

The Dales landscape has been shaped by natural forces and modified by human activity through time. The steep-sided, flat-bottomed valleys were shaped by deep deposits of glacial ice scouring the bedrock thousands of years ago. But as the ice retreated, about 12,000 years ago, the landscape gradually changed from open tundra to tree cover. It has been estimated that as the climate steadily warmed, up to 90% of the ground was covered in woodland and stocked with red and roe deer, auroch, wild pig and elk. For the bands of nomadic people who lived in this post-glacial period between 8,000 BC to 4,000 BC the main methods of food procurement were hunting, fishing and gathering fruits, nuts and berries. Finds of butchered animal bone and flint artefacts indicate that the preferred campsites of these early hunter-gatherers were located at vantage sites above the most constant high watershed springs and at the edge of open water such as Semerwater and Malham Tarn [1].

But at around 4,000 BC the change from hunting and gathering to the adoption of farming fundamentally changed the way people lived – from a reliance on migrating herds and seasonal plants to domesticating animals and growing crops. And whereas the early post-glacial landscape was largely created by natural forces, the present-day familiar Dales scenery of drystone field walls, hay barns and water meadows, superimposed on earlier historic and prehistoric remains, has been designed to meet the needs of Dales' people over the millennia.

The remains of the occupation sites of the earliest farming communities on the marginal uplands of the Training Area are slight, but due to the presence of carved rocks, burial sites and burnt mounds on the higher moors, and as a result of a major archaeological dig at Catterick, on the lowlands of the Vale of Mowbray, we do have an insight into where they built their more substantial monuments and how they expressed their religious beliefs.

Recent excavations at Marne Barracks, or RAF Catterick as it was formerly known, south of Scotch Corner, have revealed evidence of human activity alongside the River Swale during the Neolithic period, around 2,500 BC. Seventy years ago a traveller along the A1 may have had his head turned by the sight of Blenheims and Spitfires taxiing along a runway that ends close to the road. A traveller on the same route some four and a half thousand years earlier would have been equally impressed by a site of considerable size and significance constructed on this same area of flat ground close to the River Swale. In 2006 Durham University archaeologists unearthed evidence on the airfield for the existence of a double palisaded oval enclosure [2]. The palisade consisted of two concentric rings of timber posts measuring 200m and 175m on their long axes with 1,160 timber posts in the outer ring and 900 posts in the inner.

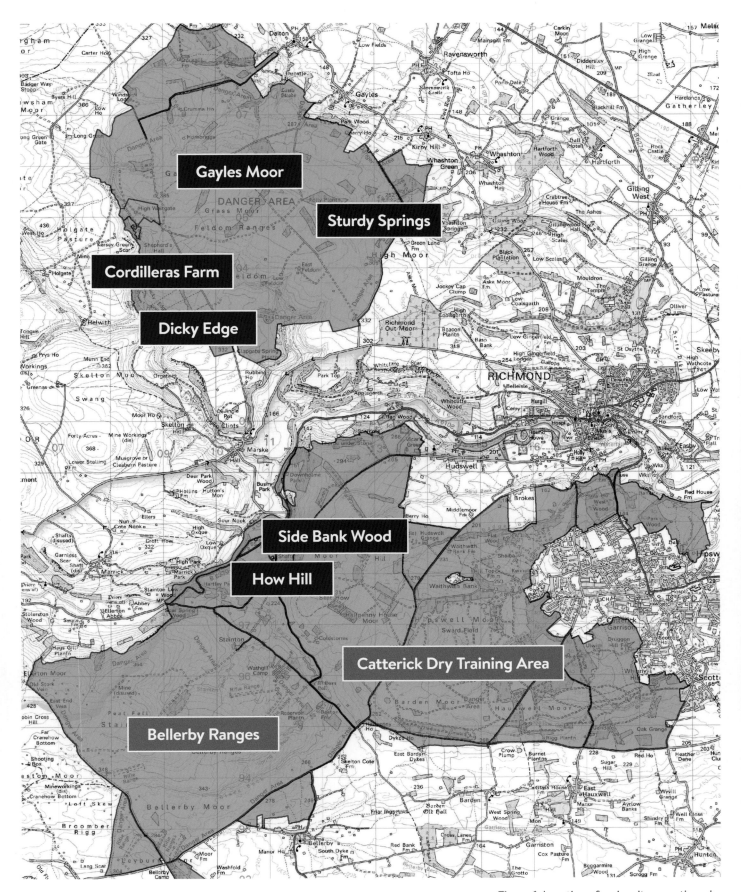

Figure 1: Location of major sites mentioned in the text (© Ordnance Survey).

1.   Out of Oblivion: A Landscape Through Time. Yorkshire Dales
      National Park Authority website (www.outofoblivion.org.uk)
2.   Hale, D. et al., A Late Neolithic Palisaded Enclosure at Marne Barracks, Catterick,
      North Yorkshire. Proceedings of the Prehistoric Society 75, 2009, pp.265-304

56

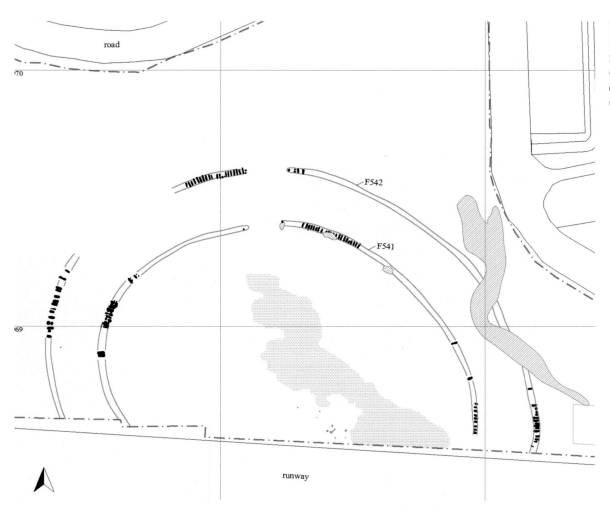

Figure 2: Marne Barracks: Plan of the palisaded enclosure excavated in 2004 (© Crown/Durham University).

road

70

F542

F541

69

runway

The archaeologists estimated that the posts stood up to 4m high and created a monument that enclosed an area of 2.75 hectares… or the equivalent to three and half football pitches! *(Figure 2)*. Although none of the timber uprights was preserved, some of them had been burnt in antiquity and the black carbon stains created a ghostly impression of the former posts *(Figure 3)*. Fortunately this material is excellent for radiocarbon dating and it has been established that the two palisades were built sometime between 2,530 BC to 2,100 BC. No obvious clues as to the function of the monument were found during its excavation but archaeologists consider that such awe-inspiring ritual structures were erected to venerate and worship the gods of the day – just as, thousands of years later, cathedrals were raised all over Europe to the glory of a Christian god. Cynics might say that the term 'Ritual' is the last refuge of an archaeological scoundrel (to paraphrase Dr Johnson) and that archaeologists use the 'R' word when they don't really know what the site was used for. But these cynics must provide a convincing answer to the question: if it wasn't a ritual ceremonial site, what was it used for?

Whilst on the subject of Marne Barracks, its origins as an airfield date back to WWI when it was established in 1915 for the Royal Flying Corps. But it also boasts the remains of a Roman villa and pottery kiln, Anglo-Saxon burials

Figure 3: Marne Barracks: Carbon residues of timber posts that once formed the oval palisade fence (© Crown/Durham University).

and a Norman motte and bailey castle within its boundary as well as anti-aircraft gun emplacements and fighter pens constructed during its days as RAF Catterick in WWII. Can it be more than coincidence that so many sites are concentrated in a relatively small area? In fact, the Vale of Mowbray, in which Marne Barracks is situated, has both a strategic and economic importance. Today the A1 takes advantage of the low-lying, flat land of the Vale, and follows the line of a major road called Dere Street built by the Romans 2,000 years ago to enable their legions and cohorts to subjugate northern England and march up to Scotland.

The impressive ritual enclosure at Marne Barracks is today buried beneath a metre of sand and gravel. To find evidence for prehistory on the Training Area, which is clearly visible under a low sun for all to see, a visit to Gayles Moor on Feldom Training Area, some 16km to the northwest of Marne Barracks, is required. Here, on an elevated windswept heather moorland overlooking the Tees Lowlands between 300m–350m above sea level, can be seen a concentration of rock art and other prehistoric sites fashioned in the Late Neolithic and Early Bronze Age at around 2,500 BC to 1,800 BC [3].

Figure 4a (above), Figure 4b (left): Gayles Moor, Feldom Range: Prehistoric carved rock showing circular cup marks (Courtesy of North Yorkshire County Council Historic Environment Team).

The rock art sites are all in the 'cup and ring' tradition and comprise relatively small earthfast rock surfaces decorated with cup marks, concentric rings and grooved figures. These enigmatic carvings range from groups of cup marks – small circular indentations, approximately 5cm diameter, pecked or ground into the rock surface – to more complex designs which include concentric circles, spirals, linear channels and geometric designs *(Figures 4a, 4b)*. Further west, on Cotherstone Moor and on the Battle Hill Training Area in County Durham, are further, similar carved rocks several of which have weathered to the point of being barely visible. In order to record the carvings for posterity 135 Geographical Squadron laser scanned the carvings most at risk. The difference between a normal image and the laser scanned image speaks for itself *(Figures 5a, 5b)*.

3.   Tim Laurie: Catterick and Feldom Conservation Group Dossier

Since the carvings are all geometric and not figurative, we can only surmise the complex meanings they held for prehistoric people 4,000 years ago. Tim Laurie has suggested that they are associated with transhumance. This is the seasonal movement of herdsmen and their flocks to summer pastures from lowland winter settlements. The carvings marked the location of familiar pastures revisited each year from early June to mid September, possibly for millennia, by family pastoral groups taking advantage of the lush summer grazing on the high limestone soils then present. The carvings have also been viewed as ritual patterns drawn by shamans or tribal magicians under the effect of drug-induced trances. The presence of similar carved motifs on the surfaces of the stone cover slabs of burials of the period does confirm their association with ideas of life and death. The detailed beliefs of the pastoralist people who made the carvings cannot be known, but perhaps the best interpretations can be made by reference to the belief systems of indigenous people of the recent past and of those who survive today.

Substantial sites such as the Marne oval enclosures required a large number of people to build them; people who were able-bodied and could be organised into efficient working groups, people who lived in communities that met their basic requirements for food, security and shelter. For very early settlers in the Mesolithic and Neolithic periods (approximately 8,000 BC to 2,500 BC) there is very little evidence on the Training Area of where such people might have lived. However, later on, in the Bronze Age period from the second millennium BC onwards, a new type of upland landscape was created. This managed landscape of parallel field boundaries survives today in Swaledale on open grouse moorland high above the limit of present pastures and has been shown to have developed during the later Bronze Age from the earliest pioneering round-house farmstead settlements. Primeval woodland was cleared by ring barking trees and small parcels of land were enclosed as paddock-like fields. Subsequently, very large areas of the upper Dale slopes were managed by parallel boundary systems, probably as sheep runs, similar to those of today. These boundaries survive as low, heather-covered stone and earth embankments, but were originally fences and later, hedgerows. The extensive coaxial field systems, as the developed early farms are called, are located on open

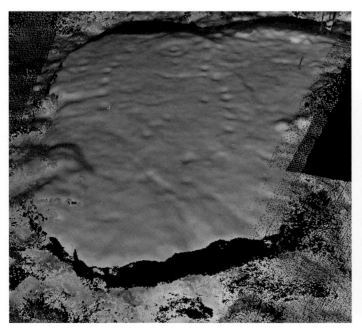

Figure 5a (left): Battlehill: Conventional digital image of a weathered carved rock (Phil Abramson, © Crown).

Figure 5b (bottom left): Battlehill: A laser-scanned image of the same rock as in Figure 5a showing the carvings more clearly – scanned by 135 Geographic Squadron RE (© Crown/Wessex Archaeology).

Figure 6 (below): Prehistoric round houses at Dicky Edge (Tim Laurie, SWAAG).

moorland between 300m and 430m on Grinton Moor, on Harkerside, on Reeth, Marrick and on Skelton Moors in Swaledale [4]. These landscapes exist in close association with the remains of earlier pioneering seasonal transhumant settlement activity in the form of small clearance cairns, irregular stone walled enclosures, round house settlements, burnt mounds, round cairns and ring cairns of earlier date. Small areas with settlements characteristic of the pioneering settlements of the Bronze Age can be seen on the Training Area on Stainton Moor and on Ellerton Moor above Juniper Gill.

Perhaps one of the most evocative prehistoric settlement sites on the Training Area survives in Marske parish at Buzzard Scar 1km to the west of Cordilleras Farm. Here, in the shelter of a limestone scar, a group of at least four conjoined round houses are visible above Throstle Gill *(Figure 6)* with the remains of an associated field system and two burnt mounds, on the open moorland above the settlement. With a little bit of imagination one can see this as a shieling or temporary settlement where these Bronze Age pastoral herdsmen lived during the summer months.

A few kilometres further south at Downholme there is evidence of settlement activity that probably started in the later prehistoric period and continued for hundreds of years into the Roman period. On a high wide terrace above Sidebank Wood and overlooking the Swale a linear settlement of small enclosed farmsteads survives along the Dale side in permanent rough pasture *(Figure 7)*. Upwards of 41 sites, including house platforms, field systems, boundary banks, field clearance cairns, possible burial mounds and a number of stones bearing cup-mark or other carvings have been recorded here. The small farmsteads and the associated field system here are likely to be of Prehistoric/Romano-British date.

A number of burnt mounds have been recorded by Tim Laurie and Paul Brown on the Training Area, and in 2005 an opportunity arose to examine in detail one of these enigmatic prehistoric monuments. The lowest of a group of four burnt mounds at Sturdy Springs on the eastern edge of Feldom Training Area in Whashton Parish was excavated under the supervision of archaeologists from Durham University [5] *(Figure 8)*. Burnt mounds, as their name suggests, comprise discard heaps of fire-cracked sandstone. They are generally oval, circular or crescent-shaped in plan and vary in size from approximately 5m-15m in diameter and 0.3m-2m in height.

4.   Laurie, T.C. et al., Coaxial Field Systems in Swaledale: A Reassessment. 2010. (www.swaag.org) website publications, Ed. Eastmead, S.P.
5.   Archaeological Services University of Durham, Sturdy Springs Burnt Mound, Feldom Range. ASUD 2007, Report 1569

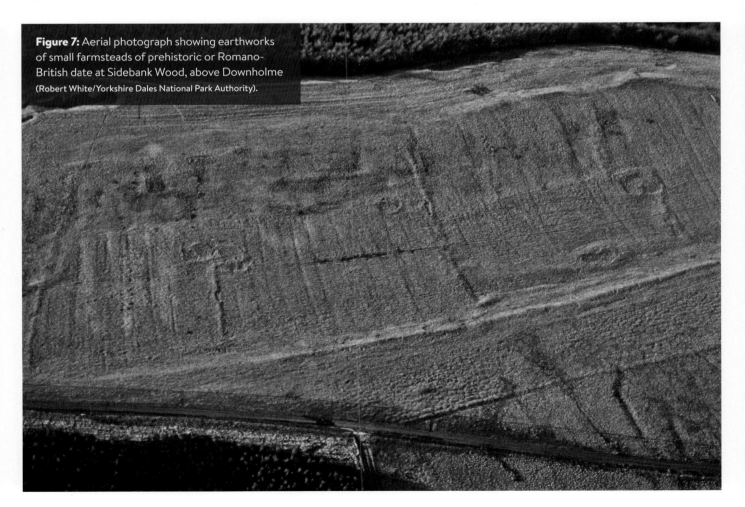

Figure 7: Aerial photograph showing earthworks of small farmsteads of prehistoric or Romano-British date at Sidebank Wood, above Downholme (Robert White/Yorkshire Dales National Park Authority).

Figure 8: Sturdy Springs, Feldom: Excavation of a Burnt Mound (© Crown/Durham University).

Burnt mounds are found throughout Britain and are among the most numerous of all prehistoric sites. Excavated examples show the mounds to be entirely composed of highly-consolidated burnt stone fragments and charcoal-blackened sand around a trough which may be in the form of a simple pit dug into impervious clay or lined with timber planks or stone slabs in order to hold water. The majority of burnt mounds identified today are found in upland locations, generally above 250m, and often next to a small stream or low energy water supply. At Sturdy Springs, this was exactly what was found and a radiocarbon date of between 1,430 BC to 1,260 BC, puts this site firmly in the Bronze Age period. The uppermost of these four burnt mounds was separately radiocarbon dated to 2,400 BC, suggesting that they were in use for a period of 1,000 years. As with many sites of the prehistoric period it is difficult to pin down the precise function of the burnt mounds. At one time they were thought to have been sites for feasting but this doesn't fit with the absence of pottery and butchered animal bones. At Sturdy Springs the fill of the trough was submitted for lipid analysis to find if there were any plant or animal residues left over from any cooking activities. The analysis found no evidence to support the use of the trough for cooking. Other interpretations are that they were used for fulling woollen cloth or making alcoholic beverages – a prehistoric micro-brewery. Yet another idea is that timbers were steamed to enable them to be worked and bent into shape. Archaeologists have now turned away from the previous interpretation of these sites as cooking places or for après-hunt feasting and prefer their use as sweat-house saunas as their most probable function. Reference to ethnography shows that the use of sweat-houses by indigenous peoples throughout northern latitudes is well documented. For example, an eye-witness account of American Plains Indian societies during the 1830s records:

'…These steam baths are always near the village on the bank of the river. They are generally built of skins…Contiguous to the lodge and outside of it, is a little furnace in the side of the bank where the woman kindles a hot fire and heats to a red heat a number of large stones…kept at these places for this particular purpose.'

Herodotus records a very similar procedure adopted by the tribes on the eastern European limit of the Roman Empire but with the use of cannabis to produce the desired atmosphere. So, if the thought of hallucinating, naked and sweaty Bronze Age men and women sharing a humid tent raises an eyebrow, you are not alone. Archaeologists too share your curiosity – but perhaps for different reasons!

Above Dalton Gill, on the northeastern edge of the Feldom Range, at Castlesteads, a steep-sided promontory between two deep, stream-cut ravines, is enclosed by a single defensive ditch and rampart bank. Castlesteads is regarded as a promontory hillfort, characteristic of the Iron Age period (c.500 BC to 50 AD). These hillforts are so called principally because they are defended enclosures built on the summit of a hill. Nowadays archaeologists tend to drop the military connotation of a fort and are more inclined to regard them as hilltop settlements. The only similar defended site within the Training Area survives in Lower Swaledale on the summit of How Hill, near Downholme village.

6. Archaeological Services University of Durham, How Hill, Downholme: Topographic, Photographic and Geophysical Surveys. ASUD 2008, Report 1834

Here, the remains of the rampart around the summit of the hill have largely been truncated by later ridge and furrow cultivation strips *(Figure 9)*. However, the early use of the hilltop was confirmed by a geophysical survey of the flat summit which revealed the ring – ditch outlines of circular structures beneath the soil *(Figure 10)* [6]. Such surveys can reveal buried features which are otherwise hidden from the naked eye. The circular features are almost certainly the foundations of circular houses some 20m in diameter with a timber frame supporting a thatch roof and wattle and daub walls. This is known from the excavation of similar buildings elsewhere. What is interesting is firstly how these circular structures have survived the later ploughing in the medieval period and secondly, why were people choosing to live on the summit of a hill, when there was perfectly suitable land on lower ground all around. Perhaps How Hill, with its wide commanding views over the Dale, could have been a military fortification, or maybe it was used as a redoubt into which the locals could have bolted at times of threat. Its use as a 'normal' hilltop settlement is always a possibility, but it is tempting to regard How Hill as a prehistoric military precursor of the modern day military Training Area.

After the Roman invasion in 43 AD of the south of England, it took almost 30 years for the Roman army to occupy the North. In spite of the presence of Roman forts commanding the river crossings at Catterick, at Greta Bridge and at Bainbridge and Wensley, Roman influence in the Dales seems to have been rather limited. Life for most of the native population probably went on much as it had done for hundreds of years before the arrival of the Roman army. There is, perhaps, more than a grain of truth in the suggestion that the main difference the Roman invasion would have made to the average person was the language

of the tax collector! With only one Roman villa in the Dales (at Gargrave) and with only slight Roman influences present at the numerous native settlements of the period, it seems as though the primary interest in the area was for woollen cloth and mineral resources – principally, lead.

Further to the east in the low-lying Vale of Mowbray it was an altogether different picture. The Romans exploited the fertile soils and guarded strategic river crossings – as shown by the remains recorded at Catterick. The Romans would have known

the settlement as *Cataractonium* and at Marne Barracks some outlying structures of the Roman settlement have been excavated including a possible villa below what is now the base's Catholic Chaplaincy, and a remarkably well-preserved pottery kiln *(Figure 11)*.

The centuries after the decline of Roman influence were for a long time called the Dark Ages by archaeologists, principally because archaeologists were very much in the dark about what actually happened during the 600 or so years between the departure of the Romans and the Norman Conquest.

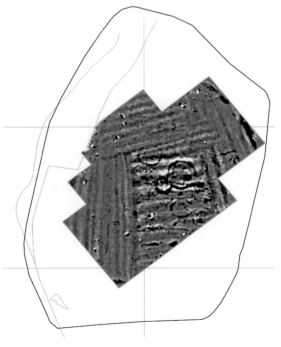

Figure 9 (above): How Hill, Downholme: Later medieval cultivation furrows crowd the slopes and summit of the Iron Age hilltop settlement (Robert White/Yorkshire Dales National Park Authority).

Figure 10 (left): How Hill, Downholme: Circular foundations of Iron Age structures recorded by a geophysical survey on the summit of How Hill (© Crown/Durham University).

As more and more sites have been recognized and excavated this situation is changing. On the relatively high ground of the Training Area two small enclosed settlements thought to be of the Viking age have been found at Dicky Edge and Far Spring Wood. At Dicky Edge the foundations of three rectangular stone buildings, with entrances in their gable walls, are located within a stone walled enclosure *(Figure 12)* [7]. On the lower ground in the Vale of York, in 1939, workmen digging foundation trenches for a new ammunition store at what was then RAF Catterick discovered building remains and a skeleton associated with a large Anglian cruciform brooch of 5th-6th century AD date. Subsequent rescue excavation revealed evidence for a total of three rooms, pottery from the later Roman period and three skeletons. The rooms may have been part of a block of buildings associated with a possible Roman villa. A further archaeological investigation was carried out in almost the same spot in 1966. Flight Lieutenant Alderson, the Education Officer at RAF Catterick, informed the Archaeology Department at Durham University that a burial with grave goods had been discovered whilst digging the footing for a signpost immediately west of the Catholic Chapel. Although the police originally removed the body and grave goods, these were later returned for study. The attitude of the skeleton and the grave goods (including 24 amber and paste beads, two pairs of copper alloy sleeve clasps and a copper alloy swastika brooch) all indicated an Anglian date for the burial. Permission was subsequently granted for a small trench to be excavated by Professor Rosemary Cramp of Durham University in order to see if the burial was part of a larger cemetery.

Figure 11: Marne Barracks: A superbly-preserved Roman pottery kiln excavated at the former RAF Catterick (© Crown/English Heritage).

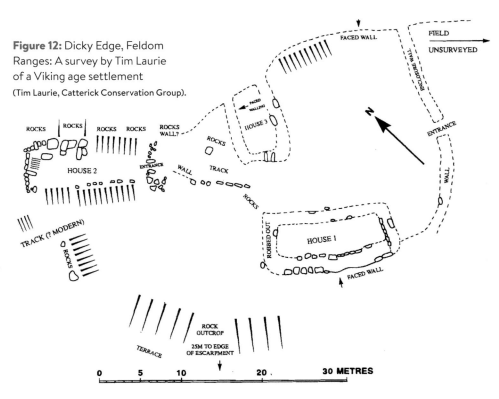

Figure 12: Dicky Edge, Feldom Ranges: A survey by Tim Laurie of a Viking age settlement (Tim Laurie, Catterick Conservation Group).

7. Tim Laurie: Feldom and Catterick Conservation Group Dossier

Forgotten Facts

A cut above the rest

It is not widely known that the skeleton of a transvestite eunuch was found by archaeologists at Baynesse Farm adjacent to Marne Barracks [8]. The young man wore a jet necklace, a jet bracelet, a shale armlet and a bronze expanding anklet and had two stones placed in his mouth. In life he would have been regarded as a transvestite and was probably a *gallus*, one of the followers of the goddess Cybele. Her would-be priests, or *galli*, castrated themselves following the example of Cybele's lover Atys, who had made himself a eunuch in her service out of remorse for his infidelity. In the castration ceremony the *galli* used special ornamented clamps, one of which was found in the Thames by London Bridge and is now in the British Museum. Thereafter Cybele's priests wore jewellery, highly-coloured female robes and turbans or tiaras and had female hair-styles. Who'd have thought it – at Catterick of all places!

8. Wilson, Peter R., Cataractonium: Roman Catterick and Its Hinterland : Excavations and Research, 1958 -1997. Council for British Archaeology 2002

Although no further burials were encountered, more Anglian metalwork finds were recovered from disturbed ground, almost certainly indicating the former presence of other burials. Further investigations were undertaken in 1994 prior to the proposed construction of a large hardstanding area and a REME workshop. The area of the workshop was found to contain part of a Romano-British field system and an Anglian sunken-floored feature or possible dwelling known as a *Grubenhaus*. Some of the finds from these sites are exhibited at the Training Area Headquarters in Wathgill Camp.

But it need not be the case that archaeology is discovered by excavation alone. The most extensive archaeological investigation on MOD land at Catterick was not an excavation but a geophysical survey of the grassed area to the north and south of the runway at Marne Barracks *(Figure 13)*. Geophysical Survey is a remote sensing method whereby extremely sensitive instrumentation can detect buried ditches, pits, wall lines and hearths that often characterize buried archaeological deposits. It is sometimes the case that a buried, hidden landscape can be revealed without having to disturb a single blade of grass. The first impression gained from the results at Marne is that the area is covered by the narrow

strips that indicate ridge and furrow cultivation of the medieval period. On closer inspection it is possible to detect other, fainter, features, which point to different phases of activity in the landscape. Linear parallel lines extend for several hundred metres in roughly a north to south direction and these are early trackways or drove roads with ditches or hedges on either side to prevent straying animals. Several rectangular enclosures may have been used to pen stock, and circular ring ditches suggest prehistoric burial or ritual features. What is perhaps surprising about the results of the survey is not the range of features which were identified but that any archaeological features at all have survived the transformation from open rural landscape in the 19th century to a fully functioning, operational airfield and army base throughout the 20th century.

There has been human activity on the land now occupied by Catterick Training Area and its environs for thousands of years. It is probably safe to assume that just as the burial mounds, settlement sites and fortifications described above are discussed and debated by archaeologists of today, then the bunkers, ranges and billets constructed by the military engineers will one day be the subject of debate and discussion by the archaeologists of tomorrow.

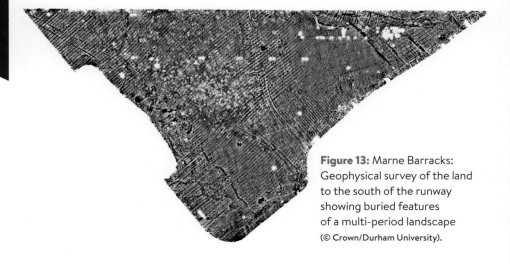

Figure 13: Marne Barracks: Geophysical survey of the land to the south of the runway showing buried features of a multi-period landscape (© Crown/Durham University).

64

Chapter 4

A Rich Seam of Industry: Geology and Mining

A Rich Seam of Industry: Geology and Mining

"Rocks are records of events that took place at the time they formed. They are books. They have a different vocabulary, a different alphabet, but you learn how to read them." — John McPhee [1]

Our planet is the library of the geologist. Understanding earth's history by reading and interpreting rock formations is as interesting to the geologist as the study of a buried villa is to an archaeologist. In fact it has been said that the geologist takes up the history of the world at the point where the archaeologist leaves it and carries it further back into antiquity. Earthquakes, volcanic eruptions, tectonic movement, sedimentation and the passage of time have, quite literally, shaped the ground on which army boots now march. Whilst the soldier, weary and cold after a day's training on windswept moorland, may not believe it, Catterick Training Area was at one point beneath a warm tropical sea, teeming with marine life! Geologist Richard Almond and mining specialist Lawrence Barker, both long-serving members of the Conservation Group, look at the ground beneath our feet.

Much of upland North Yorkshire is 'Limestone Country', where the bleached bones of the northern Pennines are visible, thrusting upwards to the west of the flat Vale of York. Catterick Garrison is situated here, at an altitude of about 140 metres above seal level and largely built on a thick plaster of boulder clay dating from the last Ice Age – which ended about 12,000 years ago. Beneath the boulder clay are the limestones which outcrop at the surface to the north and east, and the grits and sandstones which outcrop to the west, both rocks forming uplands. This solid geology dates from a much more remote period – the Upper Carboniferous of over 300 million years ago – the age when much of Britain's coal was laid down in tropical swamp forests.

During the Carboniferous period the whole area formed the margin of a vast continent which stretched northwards. Huge rivers the size of the Rhine drained into a vast shallow sub-tropical sea to the south depositing thick beds of sand and mud resulting in today's sandstone and shales. In the clear, warm water off-shore coral reefs teeming with an abundance of marine creatures flourished, forming the fossil-rich limestones which now dominate the scenery. Millions of years passed; the area was uplifted, weathered, eroded and faulted by immense earth movements. Some of the faults were injected with mineral-rich volcanic liquids from deep below the surface. The resultant copper and lead ores formed the basis of the mining industries, so important in the past economies of Swaledale and Wensleydale.

The challenging and remote nature of the terrain of the Catterick Training Area makes it particularly suitable for military training purposes. But far from it being a single landscape block we can see that the Training Area is made up of several sub-areas, each with its own distinct characteristics based on the geology, soils and vegetation.

Feldom

Feldom is probably the most interesting area geologically and scenically as the rocks are more varied and less affected by surface glacial deposits than those of the lower parts of the Training Area. This vast upland plateau, deeply dissected by fast flowing streams, reaches about 370 metres above sea level in the southwest and slopes gently towards the northeast. Limestones, often covered with a resistant flint-like rock called chert, dominate and form impressive scarps such as Dicky Edge (Figure 1). Various sandstones and thin black shales can also be seen in exposures, such as at Downholme Quarry.

The rock succession increases in age northwards from Catterick Garrison. The limestone, sandstones, shales and cherts date from the Lower Carboniferous, about 340 million years ago. The underlying, and most important, bedrock is the Main Limestone. Geologically this is located at the base of the Millstone Grit Series. In addition, important surface deposits from the Ice Age were laid down by the Stainmore Glacier.

1. McPhee, J., In Suspect Terrain, Macfarlane, Walter & Ross, 1983
2. Lokmanya Bal Gangadhar Tilak, The Arctic Home in the Vedas: An Ignored Historical Research, Sakshi Prakashan (Delhi) 1903

Figure 1: Dicky Edge Scarp
(Phil Abramson, © Crown).

The whole of Feldom has been extensively faulted by ancient earth movements and there are numerous faults and associated mineral veins crossing the area. There is a major mineral vein of lead and copper running northeast to southwest which is closely associated with the Feldom Fault. Historically, the metallic ores of lead and copper from this vein were exploited and smelted nearby then transported all over the country.

Feldom Rigg

Feldom Rigg is an outstanding example of a lateral, or side moraine of a glacier – in this case the Stainmore Ice – which moved eastwards from the Lake District over Stainmore to Feldom. The moraine marks the western boundary of the glacier and is formed from the rocks, rubble and soil that were swept aside by the ice as it gradually ploughed its way forward. The moraine at Feldom runs in a northwest to southeast direction with a steep ice-contact northeast-facing slope, and a gently dipping southwest-facing slope. In spite of subsequent weathering since the glacial retreat, Feldom Rigg is still a considerable and very visible feature, being about a 1.6 km long and 15 metres high with a distinct crest. The best view is obtained from the transmitting station to the south near Willance's Leap.

The moor to the north and east of the Rigg tends to be hummocky and is developed on boulder clay or till. This boulder clay was deposited beneath the slowly stagnating Stainmore ice. In contrast, the moor to the south and west is flatter and developed either on gravels and sands beneath the peat along the near margins of the dip slope, or almost directly on top of the Carboniferous Limestone further west. A boggy channel runs directly along the foot of the dip slope, closely following the moraine's orientation. This is the remains of a former drainage channel carrying glacial melt-water southwards to Deepdale and thus directly into the Swale Valley.

Dicky Edge

Dicky Edge, on the western margin of Feldom Ranges, is a distinctive scarp and outcrop feature facing due west across the valley of Throstle Gill, a tributary of the Marske Beck. The upper edge of the scarp lies at an altitude of 320 metres above sea level and runs approximately north to south for a distance of about 500 metres. Dicky Edge is continued structurally and geologically in the far higher and more impressive scarp feature of Orgate Scar, one mile to the south. The marine fossils at Dicky Edge show clearly that the rocks were formed under reef conditions in

68

a warm, shallow lime-rich sea on the edge of a continent – essentially a sub-tropical continental shelf sea. The more or less continuous series of scarp features of Middle Swaledale represent the southern edge of a major continent which lay to the north during the Carboniferous Period. The rock succession at Dicky Edge and Throstle Gill is fairly simple and straightforward, all the beds belonging to the Upper Carboniferous Millstone Grit Series. The succession is Main and Richmond Cherts forming the plateau surface above Dicky Edge; Main Limestone which outcrops as the scarp feature at Dicky Edge; a thin sandstone; Underset Chert; then Underset Limestone. The northern and central sections of the scarp contain two mineral veins, both lead-bearing. These are both hydro-thermal in origin, the result of metallic mineralisation from hot liquids cooling in small faults. The southerly vein trends westnorthwest to eastsoutheast and the northerly branch trends northwest to southeast. They are part of a three-pronged fault and vein system crossing Throstle Gill Valley.

The scarp at Dicky Edge is of Main Limestone but there is local variation vertically and horizontally. Although the limestone is typically in blocks, particularly in the central section where large rectangular blocks have become detached and lie at the foot of the scarp face, the limestone is not the same throughout. In the upper beds, the well-jointed limestone is locally sandy and silty, forming flags with good cleavage, useful for building and roofing. The limestone beds are full of fossils, containing the stem sections of sea lilies *(crinoids)*, shellfish which are hinged at the rear end *(brachiopods)* and the sponge spicules of *Hyalostelia smithi*. All these fossils are indications of a reef environment. A particular rich band about four metres thick of small *Spirifid brachiopods* in a silty iron-stained limestone indicates a locally poor, perhaps worsening environment. In contrast, the *Productid brachiopods* are larger, although fewer in actual numbers, and thus appear better adapted to deal with silty conditions.

The lower beds of the main scarp contain a dark grey shale band about a metre thick, appearing about two metres from the foot of the scarp. These shales are very crumbly and split easily and would have been deposited in deeper water, perhaps a trough, caused by sudden subsidence in the floor of the generally shallow continental-shelf sea. The shales are without fossils, providing a marked contrast to the limestone which is very rich in carboniferous fossils.

Cordilleras

Cordilleras, almost one kilometre to the east of Dicky Edge, is an impressive early 19th century model farmstead situated in the centre of an extensive plateau close to the southwestern edge of the Feldom Range, above the village of Marske. The plateau reflects the horizontal bedding of the solid geology which, in this area, is the Main and Richmond Chert which belongs to the Millstone Grit series dating from about 325 million years ago. Chert, the north country equivalent of flint, is a hard, blackish or dark-grey silica rock, very resistant to erosion and weathering meaning that chert beds tend to form hard capping areas in uplands. The chert around Cordilleras has a thin acid soil developed upon it which supports a sparse vegetation of scrub heather and various hill grasses. In places it has been exposed and weathered to a greyish/whitish colour similar in appearance to limestone and quite unlike pure unweathered chert which is generally dark coloured.

Downholme village

Downholme village lies roughly on the junction between sandstones and gritstones extending to the east of the village and limestones and cherts to the west. These groups of rocks belong to either the upper part of the Carboniferous Limestone Series, or to the lower part of the Carboniferous Millstone Grit Series. The scenery east and west of Downholme differs quite dramatically owing to the different characteristics of these main rock types. To the east are the poorly-drained bracken and heather-covered moors with their rolling, rounded appearance such as Downholme Moor, with Seat How at 311 metres being the highest point. To the west and northwest are the more abrupt slopes and stepped escarpments characteristic of the Carboniferous limestones and cherts, forming the east side of the Swale Valley. Again, the most important limestone here is the Main Limestone. Various sandstones and thin black shales can also be seen in Downholme Quarry.

Mineral exploitation in the village goes back to at least the Middle Ages and Arthur Raistrick refers to historical records suggesting that a mine was opened at Downholme as early as 1396[3]. The main vein, a mineralised fault extending westwards across the Swale Valley to, and beyond, Marrick runs through Downholme village. The remains of shafts, now largely overgrown and difficult to find, at the eastern end of the village, lie both on the line of the fault and to the south.

3. Raistrick, R., *The Lead Industry of Wensleydale and Swaledale*. Moorland 1975

Downholme Quarry *(Figure 2)* is now disused but was formerly an important centre for the extraction of chert, sandstone flags and lime. The rock succession is very clearly exposed in the west-facing worked face of the quarry and is as follows:

Richmond Chert	1 metre
above	
Flaggy Sandstones	2 metres
above	
Blocky Sandstones	2 metres
above	
Black Shale	1 metre
above	
Main Limestone	7 metres in thickness.

The chert, which forms a discontinuous bed at the top of the succession, is of good quality, banded in structure, and blue in colour. This rock was extracted in commercial quantities, crushed and then sent to the Staffordshire Potteries to be used as a 'filler' in the clays used to manufacture fine china and earthenware. This also was the case with the chert from the quarry in Low Bank Wood, west of Richmond Bridge.

Below the chert, the flaggy sandstones split easily to give thin slabs or flags and must have been extracted in considerable amounts for roofing purposes. Their cleavage is along thin layers of mica within the sandstone, and the flags are known to local builders as 'greybacks', despite their brownish colour!

On the west side of Downholme Quarry is a fine example of a lime kiln *(Figure 3)*. It is of substantial construction and possesses a well-made double flue which is an unusual feature of lime kilns in the North of England. The rock used in the production of lime here would have been the Main Limestone, found at the base of the succession in the nearby quarry. This kiln was apparently still in use after 1945.

Thorpe Edge

Thorpe Edge forms a spectacular north-facing scarp in Middle Swaledale, 5km west of Richmond, and is easily visible to the south of the B1068 Dale's road to Reeth beyond Thorpe House. Rising steeply from the valley floor to about 250m above sea level, it dominates that part of Swaledale, running east to west for about a kilometre from Scarcote Gill to a precipitous edge above West Wood.

Figure 2: Downholme Quarry (Phil Abramson, © Crown).

Figure 3: Limekiln at
Downholme Quarry
(Phil Abramson, © Crown).

At this point the line of the scarp turns abruptly to the south and continues for almost 2km, forming an obvious large-scale physical feature. The character of Thorpe Edge changes over this distance from steep grass-covered slopes to sheer exposed limestone blocks covered in ancient yew trees rising above steep scree slopes.

The rocks in the area of Thorpe Edge date from the Millstone Grit Series of the Carboniferous Period. Large rivers flowing into the sub-tropical sea beyond the land margin deposited the gritstones and sandstones, now found on the hilltops and in exposures. These sandy beds are found throughout the Millstone Grit Series and the sandstones in particular are a common feature of exposures in the area – already mentioned at Downholme Quarry. Strata of sandstone form an important part of the upper structure of Thorpe Edge, concealed by a soil and vegetation

cover in the east but exposed in the west and visible in the scarp face. The uppermost of these sandstones is the Ten Fathom Grit, a coarse sandy rock.

However, the most significant rocks in the area of Thorpe Edge, as regards structure, are the limestones and the cherts. The limestones vary in thickness and content; some have fossils but most do not. The knolls of limestone found within the main beds are full of fossils, particularly crinoid sea-lily stem joints, various single corals, varieties of brachiopods, and sponge debris. These characteristic fossils represent ancient coral reefs which flourished in the shallow margins of the sub-tropical sea.

The plateau surface at Thorpe Edge is covered in a thick plaster of boulder clay and other glacial drift deposited during the Ice Age. This impermeable glacial material plus the impermeable chert which underlies it both account

for the poor drainage of the moor in this vicinity, its characteristic vegetation and its hummocky appearance. Whilst this land was of little use for farming, the potential of what lay beneath the surface clearly created interest. A Y-shaped mineralised fault accounts for a series of disused bell pits and mines which can be seen on the plateau, lying to the south of Thorpe Edge following and clustered around a mineral vein.

Mining

Whilst trying to imagine and comprehend the colossal geological forces which operated over enormous periods of time, it is important to understand the relevance of these events to our own lives today. Solid rocks are the building blocks of our society, providing raw material for roads, houses, buildings and engineering projects. Mineral-rich ores have been exploited for thousands of years to make tools, weapons, structures and a whole range of objects which we take for granted. And the geological uplifts, folds and glaciers have created the canvas upon which today's Dales landscape has been painted.

Primary extraction industries such as mining and quarrying have been carried out in the Dales for hundreds of years and Lawrence Barker, a long serving member of the Conservation Group, has specialised in unearthing the history of the Dales' lead mining industry and the people who worked in it.

Veins of lead are found in the limestone as a result of upheavals that occurred millions of years ago. Faults and fissures in the limestone were filled with a mineral-rich solution that solidified to form pockets and veins of minerals – not only lead, but calcite, fluorite and barytes. Physical evidence on the ground of early lead mining is not hard to find… if you know what you are looking for. The most obvious sign of an early lead mine is a vertical circular shaft dug from the surface down to a chamber. Sometimes called a Bell Pit (although technically this was a term used in coal mining rather than lead mining), miners would follow a vein of lead down from the surface, creating a shaft which widened out after several metres. The miners would extract the lead creating a chamber at the base of the shaft. The surface evidence at the present day is often a circular depression perhaps 2m or 3m in diameter with a ring of upcast spoil around the rim. Without the aid of pit props or shoring the miners could only follow the lead ore for a short distance, so more shafts would be dug close to the first, resulting in landscape pockmarked with circular mine shafts *(Figures 4, 5)*.

The Romans exploited the mineral for their own purposes, but it wasn't until after the Norman Conquest

and the spread of the monastries that the demand for lead boomed. In the early days small-scale mining was undertaken by local men having 'rights of minery' – that is, the right to dig for ore on the wastes or commons, subject to the payment of a royalty to the Lord of the Manor. At Downholme, the development of lead mining can be traced from a single individual, Thomas De Percy, who was granted a licence to dig for lead in his field in 1396, to its widespread extraction in the 19th century. The widespread distribution of the works reflects the increased scale of mining activity which took place across the Dales from the 18th century onwards. Encouraged by injections of capital and technological developments, Britain was to become the main producer of lead in the world.

There is a long history of filling in and returning census forms since their inception in 1801 and the 1851 census was the earliest complete census to show the age, marital status, occupation and place of birth of every man woman and child in the country. This particular census period also coincides with the period when the lead mining industry was at its peak in the Dales and employment in the industry was at its maximum. In Swaledale and Arkengarthdale in 1851, approximately 2,000 people were employed in the lead mining industry; 1,200 men and boys worked underground, women and children washed and dressed the ore, as well as smelters, blacksmiths and jaggermen, who carried the ore using pack horses. Various agents were involved in buying lead and selling timber, dynamite, tools and candles. An exceptionally good wage for a miner at this time would have been about 17 shillings per week (85 pence), a woman could bring home a shilling (5 pence) a week and a boy under 14 years old could expect a penny a day (0.5p!) In bad times a miner could actually be in debt to the company as he had to buy

his own candles and dynamite and have his tools sharpened and repaired by the company or smithy. A Royal Commission report of 1864 showed that the average age of death for males over 10 was 46.7 years old, compared with less arduous occupations where the average age could be as high as 60.

Forgotten Facts

Fossilised Earth!

The body of knowledge amassed by geologists has allowed them to look not only to the beginnings of the Earth but also to its end. The history of the last geological period, the Holocene, coincides with the recorded history of mankind. To the geologist it is just a very brief moment in the long story of our planet. Gazing some 5,000 million years into the future it is possible to predict that there will be a time when the expanding sun will have caused all life on earth to become extinct and Planet Earth will itself become a giant fossil.

Figure 4: Former mineshafts on Hudswell Moor (Robert White/Yorkshire Dales National Park Authority).

Look beneath the plateau surface of Thorpe Edge and an interesting feature connected with the old mining industry can be seen. A chamber with small side-rooms has been cut into the rock face. It is entered via an open passage with a bridge over it, which culminates in an open area in front of the chamber. This strong and purposefully built man-made cave was almost certainly used to store blasting powder for the nearby lead mining and quarrying industries.

Once the lead ore had been mined it was subjected to several processes including dressing (separating the ore from the surrounding stone), crushing, hotching (sieving the ore) and bale smelting before the lead 'pig' or ingot was finally formed. An example of a smelting hearth from Downholme can be seen in the Richmondshire Museum.

The boom times of the 19th century could not last and by the 20th century cheap imports from abroad effectively killed off the lead mining industry in Britain. The last mine in Swaledale closed in 1912.

The cherished belief that the Dales landscape is one of unspoilt natural beauty is as enticing as it is untrue! Although the passage of time has softened the edges a close inspection often reveals that the impressive 'natural' scree on a steep valley slope is in fact the spoil heap of a former mine working. As Richard Almond and Laurence Barker have both clearly shown, the geological underbelly of the Dales and the Training Area has been the lifeblood of a thriving, productive, dangerous and nowadays, all but extinct, mining industry.

Figure 5: Going underground: a well-preserved level in a former lead mine at Stainton (Courtesy of Graham Newcombe).

Figure 6: A lead smelting hearth of 16th century or early 17th century date from Downholme (Courtesy of Richmondshire Museum).

Chapter 5
Living with the Army: Villages on the Training Area

Living with the Army: Villages on the Training Area

The patchwork of small communities dotted around the Training Area mainly pass unnoticed; virtually ignored and living in the shadow of the nearby garrison. To some extent this has led to the impression that they have been frozen in time; their layouts and boundaries largely preserved much as they were at the time of their purchase in the early 20th century. Yet the view that the landscape has remained unaltered over time deserves further investigation (*Figures 1a, 1b*).

The majority of the villages and land within the ancient parish of Downholme were purchased by the War Office in the early 20th century for the creation of the Catterick Training Area. However, before they were amalgamated under War Office ownership the lands within the parish had, for many hundreds of years, belonged to four separate manors. Using the Norman Conquest as a starting point, this chapter aims to explore the history of some of these villages and the communities they housed.

Setting the scene

Archaeologists and historians inform us that the land and settlements within the Training Area have been occupied for many hundreds of years, but before looking at individual villages it is helpful to consider their historical context. When William the Conqueror seized possession of England he maintained his control by redistributing the land among a hierarchy of feudal lords. By 1086 this framework of manors or landholdings was formally recognised and recorded

in the Domesday Book, the legacy of which remains today. Among these lordships was the 'Honour of Richmond' which had been created by William as a defensive post against invasions from the North. He awarded the 'Honour' to his kinsman, Alan Rufus of Brittany as a reward for his services at the Conquest, no doubt trusting that Alan would continue to serve his interests. For nearly three centuries Alan and his descendents held true to this 'Honour'. It was managed by carving up the Dale into several subordinate lordships; Stainton, Ellerton, Walburn and Downholme (the namesake for the ancient parish to which all belonged) were four such lordships.

Defensive obligations aside, activities in the early medieval period were largely confined to agricultural pursuits. The landscape at this point is one we would recognise in name only. In place of today's drystone field boundaries built to contain sheep and cattle, there were large stretches of arable land, divided into unfenced strips producing crops of cereals and perhaps flax. [1] Surrounding these were large areas of moorland – common land which could support grazing. [2] Instead of isolated, individual farms, agriculture was a much more communal, interdependent activity. As most peasant farmers did not each have enough land to support a full plough-team of up to eight oxen, they contributed one or two oxen to a shared team. Increasingly the holdings became smaller and smaller as the land was divided among the sons of the original holder. The custom, known as 'partible inheritance', meant

that property was shared by a number of heirs rather than just the eldest, leading to a pattern of smallholdings in Swaledale (*Figure 2*).

Yet, any notions of a rural idyll should be cast aside as a series of events unfolded over the following centuries which would test even the hardiest of resolves. Decline had been evident from the outset of the 14th century as poor harvests generated tax returns that were too small to support economic expansion. Crop yields fell, the result of a poor summer in 1314 and the soil became exhausted by overproduction. The following year offered no respite; weakened crops were swamped by continual rain from May until autumn the year after. Malnutrition and disease were swift in the wake with cattle and oxen struck by plague in the winter of 1319-20 from which few animals survived.

The misery felt was no doubt compounded by the background of Scottish raids the area endured at this time. The invaders, buoyed by the defeat of Edward II's forces at Bannockburn in 1314, conducted a series of attacks, tending to avoid strongholds such as Richmond and instead picking on the vulnerable surrounding areas, plundering them mercilessly. Peasants who relied on their crops and stock fled south or took to the woods with their remaining cattle at the appearance of these invaders. Any sense of victory felt when the Scots were finally defeated and driven back in 1347 was short lived. The following year bubonic plague broke out in England with devastating effect. This country-wide

Figure 1a:
Downholme Valley –
captured by the
camera (Phil Abramson,
© Crown).

Figure 1b:
Downholme Valley
– captured by the
artist (Reproduced by
permission of Winifred
Hodge).

epidemic decimated the population. In Yorkshire there were 11 graveyards dedicated exclusively to the victims of plague, one of which was at Easby near Richmond. The effect of such a catastrophic series of events was longstanding. It was not until the middle of the following century that Swaledale would once again enjoy economic prosperity.

This prosperity however, when it came, was not widely shared. Less than a century later the inequalities between the rich and the poor was one of the causes for a county-wide revolt known as 'The Pilgrimage of Grace'.

This 1536 rebellion, centred within Lincolnshire and Yorkshire, drew strength from the reaction against the changes brought about by the Reformation which had seen hundreds of the smaller religious houses (including one at Ellerton) dissolved. Some rebels claimed their actions were the result of a doctrinal fear that the spiritual welfare of the parishioners would in some way be diminished. More broadly, the feeling was that the South was in some way draining the resources of the North. Within Swaledale matters were exacerbated by a further series of bad harvests and ill-judged rent increases. Bolton

Castle resident, Lord Scrope, writing to his father in October of 1536, described how the *'commons of Mashamshire and Nidderdale had risen'* and were advancing. In particular Richard Siggiswick, Lord of Walburn Manor was targeted.

1. Fleming, A., *Swaledale.Valley of the Wild River*, Edinburgh University Press, 1998
2. The names of the moorlands which surround the villages originate back to their common land status. Thus Downholme Moor was the grazing land claimed by Downholme villagers and so on. See Fieldhouse, R. and Jennings, B., *A History of Richmond & Swaledale*, Philimore & Co. Ltd, England, 2005.

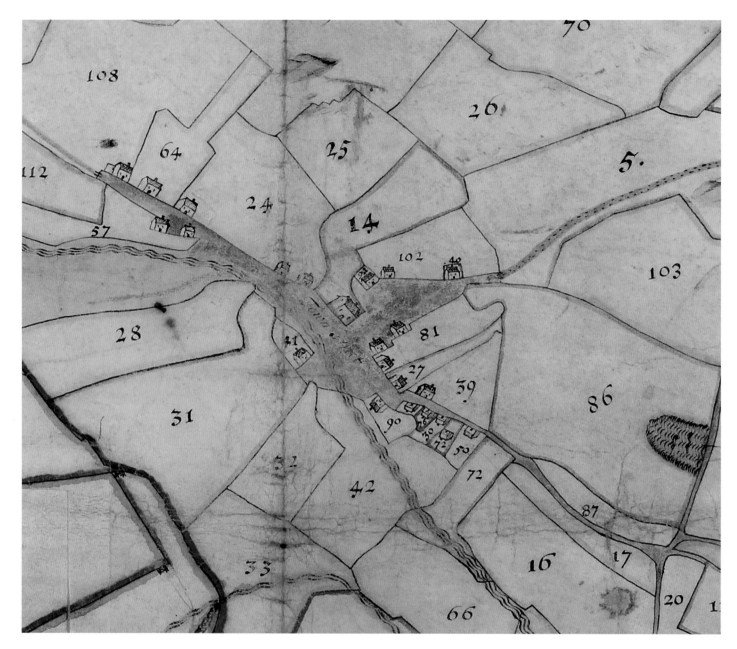

Figure 2: Stainton Manor in 1694. In Swaledale the custom of 'partible inheritance' survived into the 18th century as can be seen by the multiple small landholdings within Stainton village (Reproduced by permission of the North Yorkshire County Record Office. Ref: ZPT/26/15).

Training Area Villages: Downholme Parish

He and his predecessors had managed to force up rents faster than anywhere else in the Dale; he and others were seized, their homes and properties ransacked.

Resentment, whether religious, against taxes or the affluent South, continued to rumble on throughout the century. When Elizabeth I sought to effect a religious settlement with the establishment of the Anglican Church she continued to face anger against anything seen to be originating from London. In the end she ordered the deaths of 700 rebels, although the actual number executed was far smaller. Documentary evidence shows that many rebels, 13 of whom are listed as inhabitants of Stainton and Ellerton, were simply fined or pardoned. [3]

At the time of the Domesday Survey the parish included Downholme, Ellerton, Stainton and Walburn with 235 inhabitants, of whom about 120 were probably from Downholme. [4] Over time the populations of each had grown, reflecting the agricultural, and then industrial, success they enjoyed in turn. Yet by the early 20th century populations had dwindled and the prosperity they'd once enjoyed was mainly a memory. Nonetheless, the four settlements, although much reduced, managed to survive (*Figure 3*), and when the War Office came to make its land acquisitions, approaches had to be made to each of their manorial landlords.

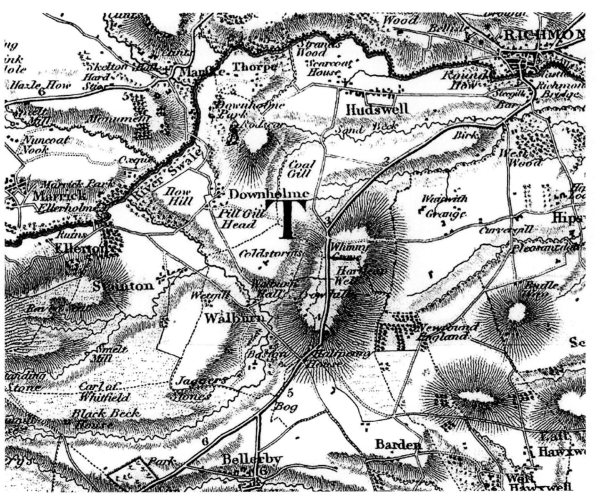

Figure 3 (left): Detail of the Teesdale Survey of Yorkshire, 1840. Downholme village can be seen at the centre surrounded by the other parish villages. The importance of mining is clearly evident on the map with abundant indications of lead mines, smelt mills and a colliery.

Figure 4a (middle): Downholme in 1904, from the moor looking down over the village (Courtesy of Clive Torrens).

Figure 4b (bottom): View of Downholme village today (Jo Haskett, Landmarc Support Services Ltd).

Downholme

The cluster of mainly 18th and 19th century houses that greet a visitor to Downholme village today *(Figure 4a, 4b)* belie its ancient credentials which stretch back to at least 2,000 years to the Iron Age inhabitants who established a hillfort or defended settlement on nearby How Hill. The fertile land around Downholme ensured that, in the centuries that followed, it remained an important social and farming centre, bolstered by the discovery of rich mineral veins beneath the ground. The plentiful opportunities for quarrying and mining this offered ensured that the village continued to flourish up until the late 19th century with the church, a school and two inns providing amenities for all the people within the parish.

3.   Le Messurier, H.S., *Downholme Historical in Downholme Valley*, Report by Catterick Garrison Conservation Group, 1 March 1988
4.   Wade, P.W., *Downholme Valley*, report by Catterick Conservation Group, 1 March 1988, editorial

A puzzling location

Before even beginning to examine the character of the village a mystery is presented. Why is the church situated some distance from the village rather than at its heart? *(Figure 5)*. The Church of St Michael and All Angels dates back to the late 12th century and is far older than other village buildings, with the exception of the ruined 15th century Downholme Hall. It is the church's Norman origins which provides a clue to its separation from the village. In the centuries following the construction of the church (c.1180) bubonic plague erupted within medieval Downholme, decimating the village's population. Buildings in the medieval period tended to be made of timber [5] which, without occupants to maintain them, soon fell into disrepair, gradually disappearing over time. Aversion to the site of such catastrophic infection may have been the reason why the following generations of builders decided to relocate the new village away from the site of the plague village. Whatever the reason, the original wooden structures have disappeared into the land leaving few, if any, visible clues to their existence.

Figure 5: The 12th century church of St Michael and All Angels, Downholme

(Jez Kalkowski, © Crown).

The Growth of a Social Centre

Given the scale of misfortune they'd faced during the 14th century it is a tribute to the hardiness of Downholme's villagers that the settlement not only survived but remained an important part of the economy in the centuries that followed. Deserted land was once more put under the plough. Where land was judged unsuitable for cultivation other uses were soon found. Keen to spot an opportunity, the incumbent manorial lord, Richard le Scrope, established Downholme Park as a deer park in 1377, realising its potential as a hunting ground.

By the 17th century a pattern of enclosure was developing, replacing the earlier practice of open field farming with its characteristic ridge and furrow cultivation strips (good examples of which can still be seen on the slopes of How Hill and at Walburn.) A 1730 map produced for the Duke of Bolton [6] shows the system of enclosure after it had been in place for at least a century. Almost all enclosed land was now being used for pasture or meadow as arable farming was replaced by livestock – which was seen as a far more profitable commodity to raise. Echoes of the old open-field farming system can be still be seen; the narrow strips indicated in Church Field, the smallest of which was a mere 10 yards wide, belonged to four different tenants *(Figure 6)*.[7]

The complicated arrangement of enclosures depicted in the map gradually simplified over time as holdings came up for disposal and were incorporated to form fewer, larger farms. This in turn led to a shift in the balance of employment and towards the growth of a class of landless labourers [8]. Census returns show that alongside agricultural labour a plethora of other trades was also established. By the 1840s butchers, wheelwrights, shoe and bootmakers all plied their trade within Downholme. In the following decades their ranks were swelled by joiners, grocers, butter dealers, blacksmiths, farriers and several journeymen. Female employment included seamstresses, dressmakers, laundresses and by the 1890s a post office and post mistress. Equally noticeable is the increase in Service as an occupation, with governesses and male and female servants listed as household members for the larger farms.

5. Manorial records for Downholme from the 12th century note the rights for inhabitants to take sufficient timber to build or repair houses. See Fieldhouse, R. and Jennings, B., *A History of Richmond & Swaledale*, Philimore & Co. Ltd, England, 2005 ed.
6. The estates belonging to the Scropes of Bolton were passed to the newly created 'Duke of Bolton' in 1689. See NYCRO ZBO
7. Fleming, A., Swaledale. *Valley of the Wild River*, Edinburgh University Press, 1998, p.66

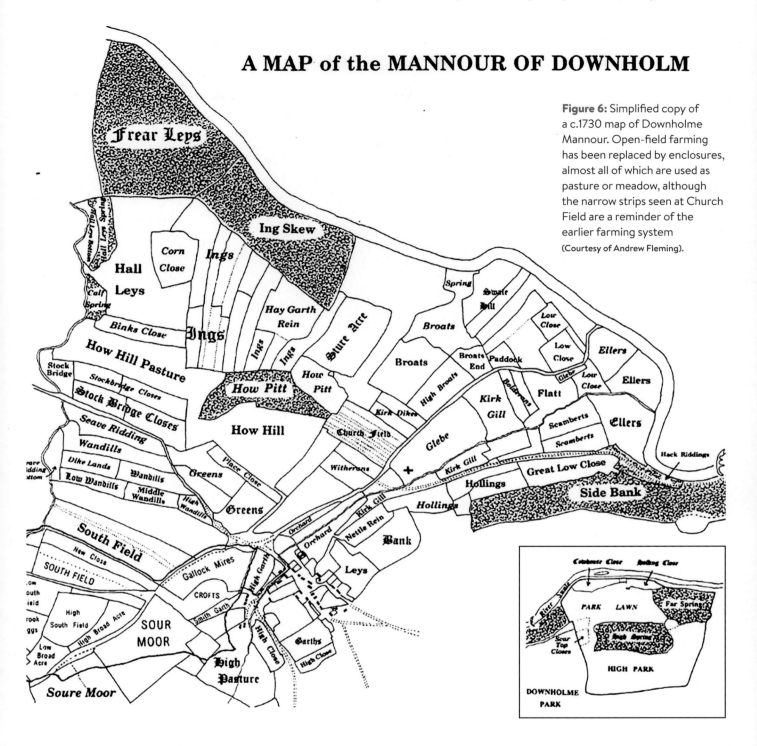

A MAP of the MANNOUR OF DOWNHOLM

Figure 6: Simplified copy of a c.1730 map of Downholme Mannour. Open-field farming has been replaced by enclosures, almost all of which are used as pasture or meadow, although the narrow strips seen at Church Field are a reminder of the earlier farming system (Courtesy of Andrew Fleming).

Buried Wealth

Research by Conservation Group member Lawrence Barker helpfully reminds us that Downholme did not owe its prosperity to agrarian success alone. Alongside those who worked on the land were those who found employment in the mines beneath. Spoil heaps provide the most extensive evidence, but the numerous quarries, limekilns and old shafts marked on maps of the area reveal the locations this once-lucrative industry. Although primarily an 18th and 19th century business there is evidence that the riches of the earth were being tapped in Downholme as early as the 14th century [9]. In 1396, a Thomas de Percy was granted a license

to dig for lead in his field. Two centuries later, in 1591, its mercantile value was clearly recognised when, among the goods listed in the inventory of Downholme resident Leonard Loftus, was an amount of itemised lead valued at £98 15 shillings [10], a figure worth close to £17,000 today.

8. Ibid. p.16
9. The rich veins of lead ore found within Swaledale have been exploited from at least Roman times onwards. Source: www.outofoblivion.org.uk/swaledale
10. The Victoria County History, A History of Yorkshire North Riding, in Le Messurier, H.S., *Downholme Historical* in Downholme Valley, report by Catterick Conservation Group, 1 March 1988, p.14

When the industry was in its heyday, several of Downholme's residents worked as either miners or quarrymen while others specialised as slate merchants, stonecutters or stonemasons *(Figure 7)* [11]. While men provided the main workforce, a fifteen year old boy [12] and even the occasional female were also employed. [13] Lead was one of the main minerals extracted, along with small amounts of copper, calcite, aragonite and barytes. At Downholme substantial quantities of chert, sandstone flags and lime were quarried. The fruits of the miners' labour yielded products that were not only used locally, but were also transported further afield, as evidenced by the account books of William Saddler, Steward to Lord Bolton. In August 1803 he wrote *'Downholme improving. The lead mines in Downholme continue[s] to grow more and more prosperous.'* Further good news was recorded in the years that followed: *'the Downholmites who yet continue to be the first in respect to profits'* he enthusiastically recorded in May 1805 *'and we have nearly 100 pieces (ingots) of their duty lead either at Hull or on the river from Boroughbridge, which may be sold on arrival.'* [14] While the mineral veins were largely worked out by the end of the 19th century there remains, to the north of the village, evidence of a lime kiln, with a double oven and chimney, which was apparently still in use up to 1945. [15] In the years before electricity came to the village, the cool interior of a mine's entrance provided a useful place for villagers to store perishable goods. [16]

Souls and Minds: The Church and The School

Parish numbers may have fluctuated during Downholme's history but St Michael and All Angels Church remains, as it has for centuries, at the heart of village spiritual life. Given its long heritage, it is no surprise to learn that the church has borne witness

Figure 7: Downholme residents James Jefferson, Percy Jefferson and Douglas Webster photographed on Back Row, Downholme village. James Jefferson worked as a slate merchant at Stainton. (Courtesy of Mrs D. West)

to several momentous events (and may well count its blessings to have survived!). From its late 12th century foundation it was, owing to its stone construction, one of the few structural survivors of the Black Death period of the 14th century. It was gifted by the Scropes to Coverham Abbey in whose possession it remained until the Dissolution of the Monasteries by Henry VIII in the 1530s. Whilst the Abbeys faced ruin the church at Downholme remained in Crown possession until it was bought by Sir Roger Beckwith of Walburn Hall in 1682 [17].

Throughout it's long history patrons have made their mark on the edifice. When the church received its Grade II★ listing in 1969 it was noted that builders of the 13th, 14th and 15th centuries had all made alterations and additions to the fabric. Three centuries elapsed until its Victorian patrons carried out three restorations during the 19th century *(Figure 8)*. Being the central church to the parish of Downholme, St Michael's serves all the surrounding villages and whereas some of today's worshipers arrive

by car, in previous centuries they would have arrived either on foot or by horse (there was reputably a stable close by for parishioners' use). In the meantime St Michael's has become quietly famous, featuring in the 1999 publication 'England's Thousand Best Churches' where it is described as *'a place of remarkable peace.'* [18]

11. By the time of the first census in 1841 mining activity as a source of employment had largely ceased in Downholme (Barker, 1992, p.24). Despite this, entries for trades associated with mining were still being recorded right up until the 1870s whilst quarrying continued into the following century
12. The 1871 census for Downholme lists 15-year-old John Peacock as a 'lead miner'
13. In April 1803 'a man and his wife' were recorded by William Saddler for managing to extract nearly half a tonne of lead ore. Barker, L., *Mineral Mining on Downholme Moor and Thorpe Edge.* Unpublished Catterick Conservation Group Report, July 1992, p.24
14. Barker, L., *Mineral Mining on Downholme Moor and Thorpe Edge.* Unpublished Catterick Conservation Group Report, p.25
15. Almond, R. L., *Geology in Downholme Valley*, report by Catterick Conservation Group, 1 March 1988, p.14
16. Interview with Doris West, 20 November 2012
17. Darrah, F.G.C., Industrial and Social in Downholme Valley, report by Catterick Conservation Group, 1 March 1988, p.23
18. Jenkins, S., *England's Thousand Best Churches*, Penguin, 1999
19. Ibid

Figure 8 (right): Funerary hatchments inside Downholme church (Jez Kalkowski, © Crown).

Figure 9 (bottom of page): Detail of 1857 1st edition Ordnance Survey map of Downholme village. Former important village facilities, including the school and the King William pub, are marked (Ref: 40YSE09NW).

While the Church was able to cater for the villagers' spiritual needs it became obvious, as the population expanded during the 18th and 19th centuries, that there were a growing number of children who also required educational provision. In 1814 a school was established thanks to the philanthropy of three Downholme-born brothers; Edward, Richard and Christopher Ellerton. Their motive, was to 'manifest their gratitude' both to the village of their birth and to God (who presumably had placed them there). Together they organised the building of a school room with a gift of £150 *'the interest to be used for instruction in reading and writing and in the Christian religion according to the Church of England, of children of poor parents belonging to Downholme and in relief of aged poor (Figure 9).'* [19]. A few years later, in 1823, landowner Lord Bolton granted a 999 year lease to the school for the princely sum of one old penny! The school continued to serve the children of Downholme Parish for 150 years before dwindling numbers forced its closure in the 1960s *(Figure 10)*.

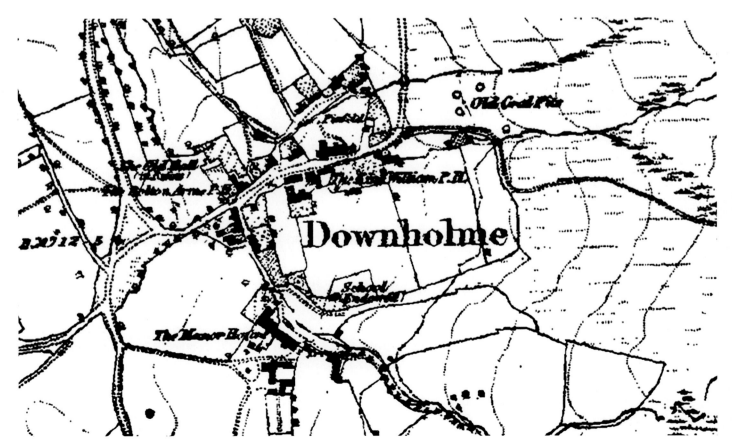

Figure 10:
Downholme School
1931. Pictured (from
left to right):
R. Dixon, J. Dixon,
J. Clemminson,
W. Brown,
D. Webster,
G. Clemminson,
E. Whitehead,
G. Brown,
H. Weller, H.Taylor,
R. Thorpe,
F. Metcalfe,
R. Thorpe,
M. Whitehead,
N. Dixon, E. Taylor,
B. Wade, J. Smith,
A. Dixon, P. Close,
M.B Webster,
M. Robinson,
Wade, K. Webster.

Welfare before the State

This vital picture of trade, industry and educational improvement shows the high level of self-sufficiency and prosperity that Downholme had once enjoyed, with population numbers reaching a peak some time around the 1820s.[20] While villagers could look to Lord Bolton as the manorial owner, an increasingly sophisticated system of governance was also set in place to ensure the smooth running of village affairs. Prior to the Enclosures at the end of the 18th century close attention was paid to managing the common pasture land. Regulations ensured that the better quality land was fairly shared and that following the winter months, a fallow period was observed to allow the grass to grow. Le Messurier carried out research into registers which relate to Downholme Parish, stretching back as far as 1768.[21] The careful tally of lists and expenditures demonstrate an impressive record of organisation and even an early form of a welfare

system. Finances were managed by a Constable who worked in tandem with a Parish Overseer to ensure that the poor and needy of the village were adequately catered for. For example, in the 1780s arrangements were made for the three orphaned Punch sisters who lived within the village. For several years they were boarded out to various individuals in the village with the villagers paying for their meat and clothes. However, as Jennings cautions, the parish's charitable actions may not have been as benevolent as first appears. In compensation for their outgoings the parish coffers received the sister's wages. No mention is made of the girls being taught any sort of trade – they were simply unpaid domestic servants, tied to labour for a master dictated by the village authorities. It was, Jennings argues, a situation akin to *'semi-slavery'* and *'The only way they could escape their lot was either to run away or get married.'*[22]

Those serving within the military could also expect financial support. In 1795 a man was given payment to

serve in the Navy *'during the war of 8 months after'* and in 1800 Militias in Downholme (nine men), Grinton (nine men) and Wensley, all received payment from the parish.

Inevitably there were those who fell foul of village law. The miscreants that were caught burning *'Thack Ling'* in 1770 were named and ordered to pay a fine of 10/6d (52 pence!).[23] By 1848 it was felt necessary to specifically appoint a committee which would deal with any nuisances that were reported. Offenders may well have faced the stocks that are rumoured to have once been situated at the top of the village.[24] Their misdemeanours may, in part, have been fuelled by another of the essentials of village life. Besides the church, school and shop, Downholme was able to boast two pubs within stumbling distance of each other. While the Bolton Arms is the sole survivor today *(Figure 12)* early Ordnance Survey maps and those residents with longer memories can recall the second pub, The King William. Furthermore it is possible

Figure 12: Bolton Arms pub, Downholme (Jez Kalkowski, © Crown).

Forgotten Facts

Downholme and Oxford; a common connection

Pupils at Downholme's school may have been surprised to know that they shared a link with scholars at Oxford University! School founder Edward Ellerton (1771-1851), was a firm believer in the principles of the Reformation with its emphasis on the value of learning. From his early education at Richmond School he went on to study at Oxford University, becoming a tutor at Magdalen College where he subsequently founded many scholarships and prizes. He is perhaps best remembered for the establishment, with his close friend Edward Pusey, of the three Pusey and Ellerton Scholarships in 1832, which are open to all members of the University. They have remained sought after prizes by Oxford University students ever since *(Figure 11)*.

Figure 11: Gargoyle at Oxford University said to be dedicated to Downholme school founder, Edward Ellerton. Edward was known at Oxford as the "The Bull" due to his large head. It is alleged, much to his annoyance, that a gargoyle, dedicated to him, was built high up on the side of a university building by some of the undergraduates.

that additional taverns once existed. A 1930s newspaper article on the village mentions the existence of the Chequers Inn and provides colourful reading with its recollection of a village feast night that took place in one of the taverns:

'At the King's Head…gin drinking went on throughout the night and on one occasion the landlord, before going to bed, tied a bucket round the neck of each of his drink sodden customers as they lay in a stupor on the bar floor. By this means he hoped to prevent them vomiting on the floor.' [25]

All change for Downholme…

Little were the villagers to know at the advent of the 20th century, the noise and activity which had filled previous years was soon to be replaced by action of a very different sort. The mechanisation of farming and exhaustion of the mineral veins by the end of the 19th century had led to a gradual shrinking in employment opportunities and in some respects the village fell into decline. The arrival of hundreds of men and machinery, when the War Office purchased the village and its environs in 1931, must have come of something of a shock *(Figure 13)*.

20. Fieldhouse, R. and Jennings, B, A., *History of Richmond & Swaledale*, Philimore & Co. Ltd, England, 2005 ed., p.258
21. NYCRO ref Z308 from Le Messurier, H.S., *Downholme Historical* in Downholme Valley, report by Catterick Conservation Group, 1 March 1988, p.15
22. Fieldhouse, R. and Jennings, B, A., *History of Richmond & Swaledale*, Philimore & Co. Ltd, England, 2005 ed., p.298
23. Ling or heather was often used for thatching or for fuel. In this case the offenders had taken ling from an area of Common land that had been designated for use as thatch or 'thack' by villagers.
24. Darlington and Stockton Times, 31 October 1936, p.10
25. Ibid

86

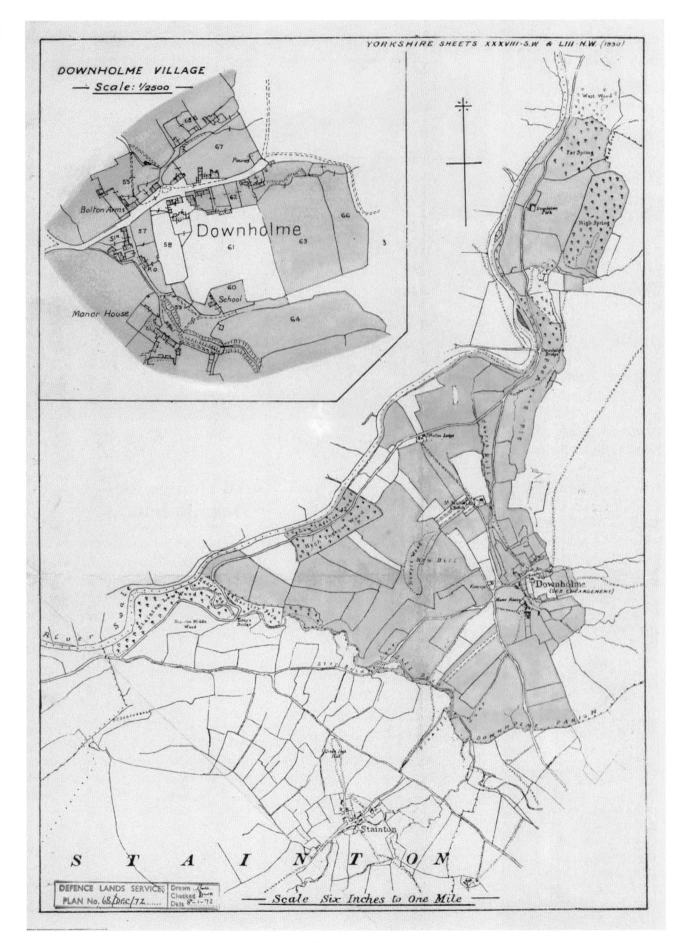

Figure 13: Map produced to accompany the conveyance of
Downholme village to the War office in 1931. The areas of land
purchased at this time are indicated in pink (© Crown).

Yet, despite the disturbance military possession brought as *'tanks, artillery and all forms of mechanical transport rattle noisily through the main street at all hours of day and night,'* the picture contemporary newspapers reported was that of an amicable acceptance by the villagers. *'Often'*, the Darlington and Stockton Times reported in 1936, *'the village is captured by an imaginary enemy after a stubborn defence involving every instrument of slaughter from a hand grenade to an aeroplane.'* But the villagers appeared to embrace the changes this brought to their rural peace. *"The military have sharpened things up a bit"* was the opinion of Downholme resident John Brown *"there is more life now than there ever has been. During the summer there is bombing going on up to 2 o'clock in the morning but we quite enjoy it."* [26] (Figures 14, 15, 16)

26. Ibid

Figure 16: A tank demolishing a dilapidated house on Silver Street, Downholme c.1930s. This cottage was in such poor repair that it was seen as safest to pull it down. Naturally, if you have one to hand, a tank is very useful for this type of job! (Courtesy of Mr & Mrs D. Calvert).

Figure 14: A Salvation Army wagon stationed outside the front of the Bolton Arms pub, 1933 (Courtesy of Mr & Mrs D. Calvert).

Figure 15: Besides tanks, men and machinery villagers also had some more unusual visitors. An elephant being exercised in a lane near Downholme, c.1940s. Possibly from a visiting circus? (Courtesy of Mr & Mrs D. Calvert).

Figure 17: Home Guard in Downholme, c.1940s. Resident Michael Webster in uniform on Silver Street (Courtesy of Mrs D. West).

Figure 18: An early picture of Wathgill Camp.

WELCOME TO WATHGILL

Present-day tenants remember *"huge manoeuvres"* taking place within the village. *"The troops were everywhere, hiding behind sheds. The exercise would go on for several days and as it went on it became obvious that they were 'capturing' the village'."* [27] Sanctuary could not be sought even within the confines of the villagers' gardens and it was not uncommon to be shocked when opening the curtains in the morning to see *"the army in our front garden with a sten gun."* [28]

Despite the restrictions being an army tenant may have brought, the War Office is generally remembered for being a good landlord. *'Within the three or four years since the War Department acquired Downholme the village has undergone a great transformation'* 1930s newspaper readers were informed *'which has given the inhabitants the incentive to pride of occupation.'* [29] The village is recalled as being in a state of disrepair at the point of the War Office purchase. Cases such as the collapsed ceiling of the Calvert's family home at Downholme Manor were not unusual and, where possible, repairs were made. A home guard was formed within the village, with meetings taking place in the village pub *(Figure 17)*. In times of extreme weather when severe snowstorms cut off the village enthusiastic troops did their best to assist, skiing over with provisions, although even they could not assist the unfortunate residents of one house whose location at the top of the village meant it bore the brunt of snows drifting off the moor.

Forgotten Facts

Grave Concerns

No Victorian tale is complete without a degree of tragedy and melodrama and Downholme Parish seems to have provided plenty of both for contemporary writers to work upon. Tragically, in the 1880s, two suicides occurred within a few years of each other. The first was 32 year old gamekeeper Eli Ride, resident of Crow Hills who was found hanging by the sycamore tree outside his property. Keen to furnish readers with a dramatic picture, the contemporary newspaper report describes the heartbreaking discovery by his young son who had found his father's body a few yards away and facing his bedroom window *'hanging in a stooping position with a small faithful Spanish dog crouched at his feet.'* [32] Equally disturbing was the death of the Downholme vicar, the Rev. A. Clark in 1883. Although less floridly described his suicide is no less gruesome. The Reverend was found with his throat cut and the pair of sharp scissors he had used nearby. [33]

On a less sombre note the reported exploits of Downholme resident Dick Ellerton demonstrate that planning for one's departure was a serious business. Mr Ellerton was reportedly *'a man of tremendous proportions whose hat was as big as an umbrella.'* This weighty issue seems to have sat heavy on his mind as well as on his frame. Once he had overseen production of the coffin which would later accommodate him, he tasked four men to carry it *'just to satisfy himself that his own funeral would be undertaken with dignity and decorum.'* [34]

The boyhood memory of one former resident recalls that such was the depth of drifts on one particularly harsh winter in the 1950s, *"that had it been solid enough I could have stepped out onto it from my bedroom window."* His father, meanwhile, on confronting the solid wall of snow that greeted him as he opened his front door, realised his only means of escape was to create a tunnel by shovelling the snow into the passage way of the house! [30]

In general the consensus seems to have been that the army's presence outweighed any inconveniences it may have caused. Put simply *"Far better that it's 'our' lads then any others."* [31]

How the residents in this century will feel remains to be seen. In 2012 Downholme was sold and although the village no longer falls under military ownership the lands which surround it continue to serve as a training ground for tomorrow's soldiers.

27. Interview with David and Jean Calvert, 7 December 2012
28. Interview with Doris West, 20 November 2012
29. Darlington and Stockton Times, 31 October 1936, p.10
30. Interview with John Joe Pettit, 18 December 2012
31. Interview with Doris West, 20 November 2012
32. Northern Echo, 13 January, 1880; Issue 3117
33. Lloyds Weekly Newspaper, London, 8 July, 1883
34. Darlington and Stockton Times, 31 October 1936, p.10

Figure 19a: Aerial view of Walburn Deserted Medieval Village. The outline of the tofts and crofts can clearly be seen on either side of the stream (Robert White/Yorkshire Dales National Park Authority).

Figure 19b (right): Aerial view of Walburn. Although the medieval village does not appear on this photograph, the outlying ridge and furrow cultivation strips seen in the surrounding fields were formed by medieval ploughing (Robert White/Yorkshire Dales National Park Authority).

Figure 20: Sketch plan of the deserted medieval village of Walburn (Courtesy of Andrew Fleming).

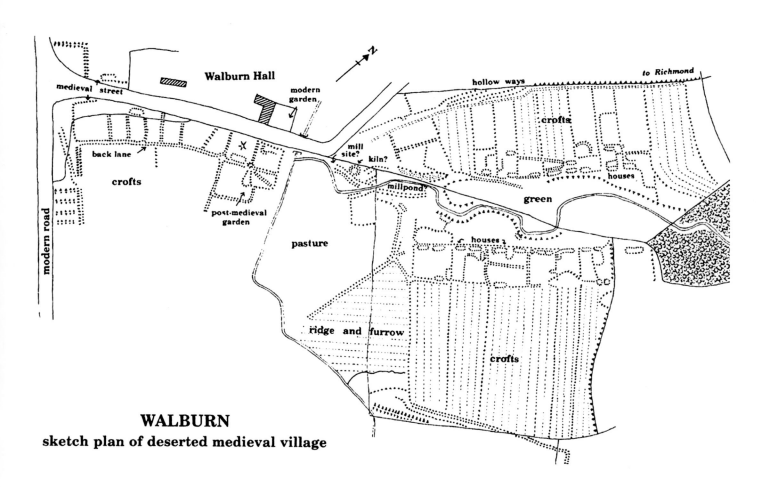

WALBURN
sketch plan of deserted medieval village

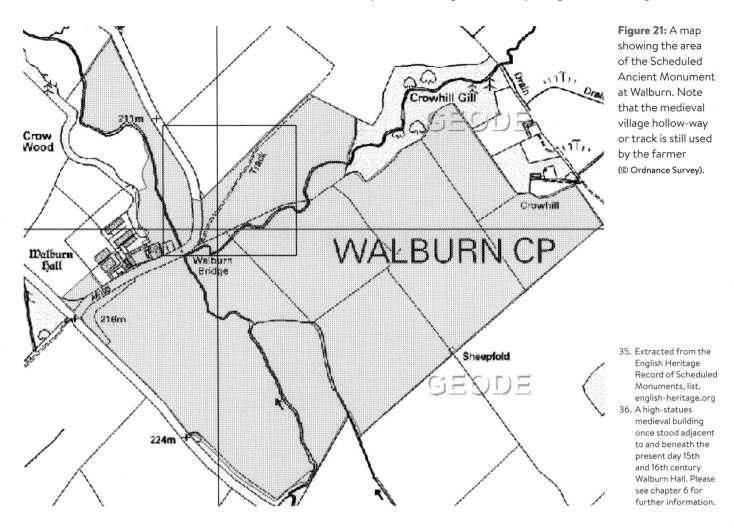

Figure 21: A map showing the area of the Scheduled Ancient Monument at Walburn. Note that the medieval village hollow-way or track is still used by the farmer (© Ordnance Survey).

35. Extracted from the English Heritage Record of Scheduled Monuments, list. english-heritage.org

36. A high-statues medieval building once stood adjacent to and beneath the present day 15th and 16th century Walburn Hall. Please see chapter 6 for further information.

Walburn

In the pasture fields adjacent to Walburn Hall, there once stood a thriving medieval village. A glimpse is afforded from above, where the outlines of the buildings which once clustered in the fields to the east of Walburn bridge are faintly visible on aerial photographs *(Figures 19a, 19b)*. The first written account of Walburn village was in 1222 but is quite likely, given that it follows a layout used in earlier Norman settlements, that it was built during the late 11th or early 12th century *(Figure 20)*. [35] Archaeological research has revealed a carefully planned village with two rows of buildings facing each other across a wide village green with a street and stream or 'gill' at its centre. Nowadays the stream follows a meandering path but in medieval times it would have been canalised and its head (now swathed under a sycamore plantation) would have supplied the villagers with drinking water.

The buildings which lined the village street stood within a set of regular enclosures known as 'tofts' which contained dwellings and other buildings in a small yard. To the rear an extension of land, known as the 'croft', acted as an individual small-holding. Whilst the main body of the village lay to the east of Walburn Hall, the village street formed a right angle with the bend of the modern road, it also extended further west, crossing over Gill Beck with tofts standing opposite medieval Walburn Hall. [36] The present day road now occupies the stretch of land which had formed the village street. Behind the crofts on the northern edge of the village there are the remains of the hollow way which would have provided the medieval route into Richmond. Modern maps reveal that this ancient trackway – although it now only extends as far as the woods behind Crowhill Farm – is still in use today as a farm track *(Figure 21)*.

Surrounding the village were Walburn's extensive outfields which show up well in low sunlight or when snow is melting. These large un-enclosed arable fields were divided into strips which were allocated to individual tenants. Cultivation of these strips, using teams of oxen to pull heavy ploughs, created the long ridges and furrows, which are still visible today. In common with other villages within the parish Walburn was also hit by the misfortunes in the 14th century, courtesy of bad harvests, disease and raids by the Scots. While it didn't bounce back in the manner of its neighbouring village at Downholme, it did sufficiently regenerate to provide a model of organisation. Evidence uncovered by Le Messurier demonstrates that a sophisticated farming plan of 'cropping' was in place by the 15th century. This system divided the village land into

Figure 22 (top):
A pool at Boston Farm, Walburn, created to provide drinking water for the horses stationed at Wathgill Camp
(Jo Haskett, Landmarc Support Services Ltd).

Figure 23 (bottom):
The hamlet of Stainton nestling amongst the hills
(Phil Abramson, © Crown).

three areas, two of which were cultivated (spring and winter crops) while the third remained fallow. This arrangement ensured that the land was put to the best collective use and could provide for the village all the year round. [37]

Perhaps it was this level of organisation which allowed for Walburn's early adoption of the enclosure system which seems to have been taking place well ahead of the 16th century benchmark assumed for other nearby villages. As early as 1495 Humphrey Segiswick was granted a close within Walburn. [38] Further enclosures were swift to follow so that less than a century later the rental records of 1586 show 1,133 acres lying in 33 closes. [39] These changes didn't prevent some elements of the older style of farming to remain. In an echo of the communal strip farming some of the new closes were held in multiple occupation. Further subdivision over the following centuries meant that by the early 18th century the number of fields had doubled from 33 to 62 and by 1820 to 120 fields. [40]

From this peak of land-holding in the early 19th century the following years saw this number decrease. Just as the village had witnessed a rapid transition to enclosure, the step towards fewer, larger farms seems equally as swift. By the mid-century the land had sufficiently consolidated to form five large farms: Walburn Hall, Boston, Coldstorms, Crowhills and Wathgill *(Figure 22)*. As the century progressed the village continued to shrink to the extent that Whellan, when he wrote a history of the area in 1859, described it as a 'hamlet' with a population of only 33. [41] Nowadays the first four of those 19th century farms still remain within farming hands. The fifth, Wathgill, now finds itself adjacent to the army's northern headquarters complex and the land which had once been tilled by a medieval farming community now serve as part of the Catterick Training Area. [42]

Stainton

Today the hamlet of Stainton could easily pass unnoticed, accessible only by a single road leading off the Richmond to Reeth road *(Figure 23)*, while the moorlands which surround it are perhaps more widely recognised as one of the army rifle ranges. However, the discovery of manorial court records from the late 17th century reveal it to have once been a surprisingly lively and large community, perhaps numbering up to 40 families *(Figure 24)*. [43] These records, managed by the Steward, document the activities of tenants at Stainton Manor and give us a sometimes colourful insight into the affairs of this vibrant rural community. Courts at Stainton were normally held twice a year and 90 individuals who came up before the Court

Figure 24: *'A Map and true Survey of all the Inclosed Ground in the Lordship of Stainton...Anno Domini 1694'.* By the late Middle Ages the majority of villages within Downholme parish were partially or wholly deserted but Stainton, as this map shows, was an exception. In 1694 it had several houses and all those who farmed the land lived in the village. Their names are listed alongside the enclosures they held in the table shown on the left side (Reproduced by permission of the North Yorkshire County Record Office. Ref: ZPT/26/15).

from May 1653 to October 1672 are known. Dealings with inhabitants known as 'inmates' and 'undersettles' seem to have provided a lot of the Court's business. Such persons, who appeared not to have contributed financially to the lord, were seen as a burden on the resources of the township and efforts were made to remove them by using enforcements and heavy fines. Being a relative of a town tenant offered no protection. For example, in November 1665 tenant William Myers faced a fine of 10s if he didn't remove his mother, Ann Myers, out of town within four days. Likewise, young married people were not allowed to live in their parents' house or another house in the same tenement. Squabbles between legitimate tenants also provide colourful reading. In April 1659 a Michael Jackson prosecuted three neighbours for trespass, alleging that their beasts had eaten his corn. The subsequent retaliation by one of the neighbours attracted a 10s fine *'for giveing uncivill speeches in open court , namely that he cares not for any screwing fellow that comes to screw up men, he cared not a fart for them, with any uncivill language.'* Not content with just one action, Mr Jackson brought actions for debt against a further five inhabitants along with several cases of assault. In 1664 his wife Elizabeth, seemingly unwilling to let him dominate the limelight, also added to the jurors' burden by throwing a stone at her neighbour, Ursuley Robinson, after the latter had called her a *'miller whore.'*

Sadly, no further court records have been found beyond 1734 but the exploits of the Scrope family, the lords of the aforementioned Stainton Manor, provide interest for the rest of the century. Whilst the manorial courts were busy dealing with the bureaucracy (and squabbles) of village life the lords focused their attention elsewhere, namely on the promise of the mineral riches that their moorlands might offer *(Figure 25).* The family member recorded as having an interest was Simon Scrope . In 1680 he is said to have *'discovered a lead mine in part of his estate at Stainton and apprehending the same might be of great advantage to his family if the same were duly wrought and carried on did enjoyn his son and heir apparent Simon Scroop (sic) to carry on the same.'* [44]

37. Le Messurier, H.S., 'Downholme Historical' in *Downholme Valley, report by Catterick Conservation Group*, 1 March 1988, p.10
38. Ibid, p.13
39. Ibid
40. Ibid
41. Whellan., *The History of Yorkshire and North Riding.* 1859
42. The Medieval Settlement and Field System at Walburn Hall was first scheduled on 10 October 2000
43. These records are now deposited in the North Yorkshire County Record Office, reference ZPT 3. Initial research into the records was made by Ashcroft, M.Y. and published as The population of Stainton (by Downholme) in the middle 'of the 17th century in the *Cleveland & Teesdale Local History Society*, Bulletin 16, 1972
44. *The Scropes of Danby*, reference guide held in North Yorkshire County Record Office, p.12

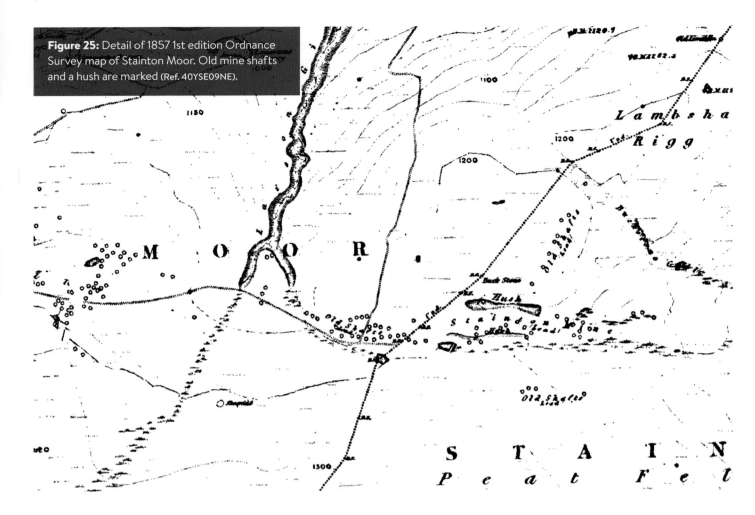

Figure 25: Detail of 1857 1st edition Ordnance Survey map of Stainton Moor. Old mine shafts and a hush are marked (Ref. 40YSE09NE).

When he succeeded his father in 1691, Simon Scrope II seized his mining suggestions with great enthusiasm. Not content to confine his exploits to the mines of his Stainton estate, he additionally invested in mining ventures further afield into the North West and Teesdale. Unfortunately his business skills did not match up to his ambitions and by 1714 he was deeply in debt. Relatives from his extended family were forced to come to the rescue in order to prevent his imprisonment and the indiscriminate break-up of the family estates. A private Act of Parliament was hastily negotiated. Simon, keen to excuse his financial failings, cited inherited debts and his hopes of realising his father's lead mining aspirations as the cause. Not surprisingly he was less keen to mention that his extravagant tastes and devotion to fashionable pastimes such as cockfighting, may have also largely contributed to his predicament.

Whether they believed his excuses or not the Trustees of the Act kept a close eye on Simon's expenditures in the years that followed. It was an intuition for which they were no doubt grateful as Simon showed no let up on his spending, incurring yet more debts. Eventually his extravagant lifestyle seems to have caught up with him and he died in 1723 aged only 57, leaving his son Simon Thomas Scrope as his 14 year old heir. Given his youth the estate affairs were initially managed by Simon's uncle, William, before he was able to take the helm. Under his guidance mining activities on Stainton Moor appear to have flourished. Initially he focused on coal-mining [45] but by the 1740s he had turned his attention to lead mining. From 1742-1747 *'it is probable that over £2,700 worth of lead, representing over 225 fothers or 247 tons, had been produced and sold from Stainton Moor mines.'* [46]

Figure 26: A mine 'shop' on Stainton Moor, used as a shelter by workers in the lead mining industry (Jo Haskett, Landmarc Support Services Ltd).

While this was an encouraging figure, Simon III realised that his true profit could have been higher were it not for the innumerable additional expenses mining incurred such as smelting and carriage of the lead. The idea of constructing a local smelting mill on Stainton Moor had been initially suggested in 1754 but it was not until the 1780s that it was finally constructed. [47] Whether or not he had an a suspicion that the productive years for Stainton mines would soon be over, Simon must have felt some satisfaction in his final years to cast his eyes over his successful mines, complete with smelting mill, and to realise that his grandfather's wishes had at last been realised to their full potential *(Figure 26)*.

By the 19th century the flurry of mining activity on the moorland began to gradually decrease with only small-scale quarrying for flags and slates. Apart from occasional mentions in histories of Downholme Parish [48] there is little written evidence of Stainton's declining population until the census in 1841 which officially confirmed this fact. These returns, while perhaps providing more accessible and reliable statistics, sadly fail to give the vivid picture of life that the earlier records had achieved.

Ellerton Abbey

Curious travellers on the Richmond to Reeth road may wonder why a lone church tower stands in one of the fields set back from the road *(Figure 27)*. These picturesque ruins date back to the 12th century when they formed a part of Ellerton Priory. Their ruinous state – only a portion of the west tower and a few walls of the church building now remain – bear witness to the effects of the dissolution and centuries of neglect.

45. In 1743 a 21 year lease for coal mining on Stainton Moor was set up with a group of three gentlemen from Middleham, Marrick and Leyburn. Extracted from: The Scropes of Danby, reference guide held in North Yorkshire County Record Office, p.13
46. Ibid. p.14
47. Ibid. p.17
48. Whellan's 1859 history of the area glumly records that there is 'a grey flag slate quarry worked by William Naylor' and 'a lead mine worked since 1856 but is not very productive'. The population is said to be 40 persons From *The History of Yorkshire and North Riding*, Whellan, 1859

Figure 27: The ruins of Ellerton Priory and nearby Ellerton Abbey house (Jo Haskett, Landmarc Support Services Ltd).

At the time of the Norman invasion the Saxon lord Gamal received tax for the '2 carucates of land'[49] Ellerton held, before the manor then passed into the ownership of Count Alan in 1086. When the priory was founded a century later by Warnerus [50], chief steward to the Earl of Richmond, the lands then passed into the priory's ownership [51] which, according to Fleming, once formed part of a (now deserted) village. [52] The priory's inhabitants were a community of Cistercian nuns. Despite its small size and spare endowment it still managed to attract the attention of the Scots who, on one of their predatory incursions into Swaledale during the 14th century, sacked the nunnery and carried away several charters and writings. Undeterred, the hardy nuns remained *in situ* for nearly another century but were finally defeated when the Dissolution came in 1536 and Johanna Harkey, the last prioress, was forced to surrender the lands to Ralph Closeby of King Henry VIII's household. By 1601 it passed onto the Drax family who, in 1830, built the Regency villa situated within the former priory grounds, calling it 'Ellerton Abbey'.

From this point ownership of the land passed in uninterrupted succession…that was until the 20th century and the arrival of a rather different sort of invader, this time in the guise of War Office officials! Fortunately for the Erle-Drax family, they sought to neither raid nor ruin their house, but merely to expand their army landholdings with the purchase of the adjoining moorland in 1926.

Training Area Villages: 'Turf Wars'. Bellerby, Barden and Halfpenny House

While Bellerby does not form part of Catterick Training Area, sections of the moorland which surround the village do. Bellerby Moor has formed an essential part of Catterick's Training Area from as early as 1928, initially accommodating the Brigade Musketry Camp. The camp has since been dismantled and relocated at Wathgill [53] but the Training Area remains, bordering Stainton, Barden and Walburn Moors *(Figure 28)*.

Historically a moorland's name indicates the village which assumed ownership. As nature, or ancient rights, would have it these divisions were not equal. Those villages which held more barren moorlands could count vast stretches of land as their own but those villages whose lands fell in the more fertile parts of the Dale had to settle with considerably less. Disputes over land ownership and the extent which each manor could claim frequently occurred. Such was the case with Walburn and Bellerby whose inhabitants seem to have had a particularly quarrelsome relationship when it came to the matter of claiming 'ones turf' (or moorland in this case!). Pre-enclosure records paint a comic picture of night-time hide-and-seek where Bellerby tenants:

'from time to time drove & hounded off the Wawbon (Walburn) cattle – on Bellerby Moor & very often went thither on purpose to do so & have seen Wawbon tenants…hide themselves from being seen with their cattle and used by stealth in the night to putt their cattle on.'[54]

A further source of grievance was the cutting of firewood in a coppice close to Bosdale Gate by Walburn tenants who claimed that their one penny per household 'smoke money' allowed this – a claim disputed by Bellerby's incumbent lord of the manor, Mr Metcalfe. [55]

The lords themselves were not above quarrelling with each other. A legal dispute of 1725 saw John Metcalfe pitched against Sir Roger Beckwith of Walburn, over the boundary between Skelton Cote (within Bellerby territory) and Boston Farm (in Walburn Manor). Beckwith asserted his right to the land with ancient grazing rights, apparently issued by William de Bellerby. The dispute was resolved, somewhat unusually, by the fate of the Bellerby resident, Mary Moreland, whose grave lay at the centre of the disputed ground. This unfortunate lady hanged herself in the 1690s and had been buried on the moor, her suicide denying her a space within consecrated ground. Her final resting spot was intended to be well within the Bellerby lands but instead ended up in a 17th century no-mans land after the bier carrying her body broke. Her panicked bearers, apparently conscious of *'the way she stank'* and so *'thinking no harm they buryed her where the stey broke.'*[56] This spot, although 40 yards short of the actual boundary near the Richmond Road, became a boundary point in folk memory. Today it is marked by a rather innocuous spring but nevertheless, it was essential in resolving the lord's dispute which had reached the York Court of Assizes *(Figure 29)*. [57]

49. A 'carucate' was the amount of land tillable by a team of eight oxen in a ploughing season and was used as a unit of tax assessment
50. The assorted histories of the area have given various derivatives of the name for the person said to be the Priory's founder. Besides Warnerus these have included: Wymer, Whymerus, Wymor, Warnerius and Warner
51. Extracted from *Parishes: Downholme, A History of the Country of York North Riding: Volume 1* in Page, W., ed. Victoria Country History, 1914, pp 225 – 232
52. Today only Swale Farm remains from the former Ellerton Village. See Fleming, A., *Swaledale. Valley of the Wild River*, Edinburgh University Press, 1998, p.105
53. Bellerby Camp was dismantled soon after Wathgill Camp opened in 1983.
54. NYCRO, ZDX 130 – 4 in Hall, D.S., *Bellerby: A Dalesend Village*. 1989, p.22-23
55. The Metcalfe family bought the manorial rights in c.1570. They retained it through at least seven generations.
56. NYCRO, ZDX, 132 – 33, ZAW
57. Le Messurier, H.S., *Downholme Historical in Downholme Valley*, report by Catterick Conservation Group, 1 March 1988, p.13

Figure 28: An early postcard of Bellerby Moor from the 1920's (Courtesy of Clive Torrens).

So matters may have continued on were it not for the arrival of enclosures in the late 18th century. Landowners were invited to stake their claims at public meetings and commissioners were appointed in an Act of 1770 to measure, value and distribute the land. Finally in a bid to resolve any quibbles an Act of Parliament divided the moorland shared between Walburn and Bellerby, granting John Hutton (who was now the lord at Walburn) 453 acres to incorporate within his farm.

Close to the disputed moorlands is Halfpenny House, whose buildings act as a far more substantial and satisfactory indication of boundary division than poor Mary Moreland's Spring could ever have hoped to achieve. Unfortunately for the 18th century Commissioners involved in the Walburn/Bellerby dispute, Halfpenny is close, but

not close enough, and instead marks the boundaries of two other moorlands. Fate has decreed that the busy road which crudely divides the complex of buildings that make up Halfpenny House and farm means that the detached outbuildings on one side of the road sit within the parish of Downholme while the farmhouse falls within Barden *(Figure 30)*. Halfpenny's role in local history is more significant than simply a convenient border marker. It is situated on the Richmond to Lancaster turnpike road of 1751 and, as its name implies, Halfpenny House was once a tollhouse, the half-penny being the ½ d toll to get to Richmond *(Figure 31a, 31b)*.

Links between the communities had of course existed long before the arrival of turnpikes, perhaps dating as far back as Roman times. Over time, as settlements and markets

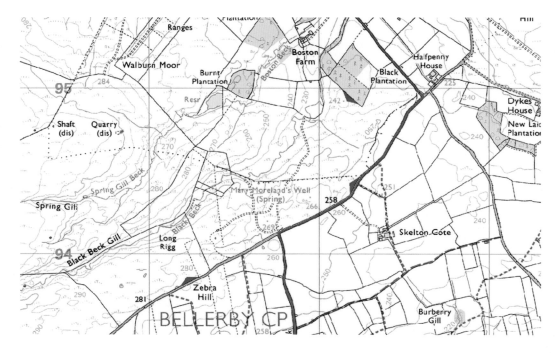

Figure 29: Detail of a modern Ordnance Survey map showing the site of Mary Moreland's Well or Spring (© Ordnance Survey).

consolidated, a network of local trackways began to form, with Richmond, which was granted a market charter in 1155 in the reign of Henry II, at its centre. By the medieval period longer distance routes were becoming more necessary. Long trains of packhorses would have become an increasingly familiar site carrying loads of wool, lead and coal to markets outside the area and bringing back necessities such as salt. Packhorses were particularly important to the area's burgeoning lead industry as they were the most efficient method of transport to and from some of the more remote mining areas. Longer journeys required overnight stabling and a room for the train leaders (known as 'Jaggers') and a series of Stage houses were established along the route to meet this need. In its early years Halfpenny House may have served this purpose given that its construction date of 1728 predates the turnpike road by more than 20 years.

As industry and heavy loads increased it became clear that the packhorse routes were not adequate. Hard-surfaced roads, passable all year round, were needed to transport wheeled carts and wagons. The solution came in the 18th century with the establishment of the Turnpike Trusts which allowed private entrepreneurs to build and maintain turnpike roads, extracting tolls from the travellers who used them in order to recoup their costs and also make a profit.

For those manning the gates at Halfpenny House its strategic position and facilities offered something of a golden opportunity for fare collection. Tolls and traffic arrived not only on the turnpike road to and from Lancashire but also from those using the Richmond to Reeth turnpike road which was situated close by. Further profit could be realised thanks to Halfpenny's former status as a licensed inn offering travellers the opportunity to enjoy extremely local ale, courtesy of the in-house brewery located opposite (Figures 32a, 32b).

Some of the principal users of the road would have been the Downholme parish villagers, to whom the export trade was especially important during the industrial boom years. The roads themselves provided employment, and jobs associated with transport appear in almost all of the parish censuses. The blacksmiths, farriers and wheelwrights that are listed would have ensured that beast and cart alike were fit for

purpose while a 'stone-breaker for road repair' would no doubt have paired up with the two 'road-repairers' that were listed on the 1901 census.

From the late 19th century the county councils took over the running and repair of the county road system. The Turnpike Trusts were dismantled and as industry declined across the Dales, the residents of Halfpenny House might have expected road use to have quietened. The arrival of Catterick Camp in the early 20th century soon dismissed any such notions. Swift access was needed to the newly-established training areas on Barden, Bellerby, Stainton, Walburn and Downholme moors. Plans were being made from the early 1920s for a new road to directly connect the training areas with Camp centre. By 1925, once the necessary formalities of land conveyance had taken place, construction of the Range Road began in earnest, crudely slicing through moor and farmland alike (Figure 33).

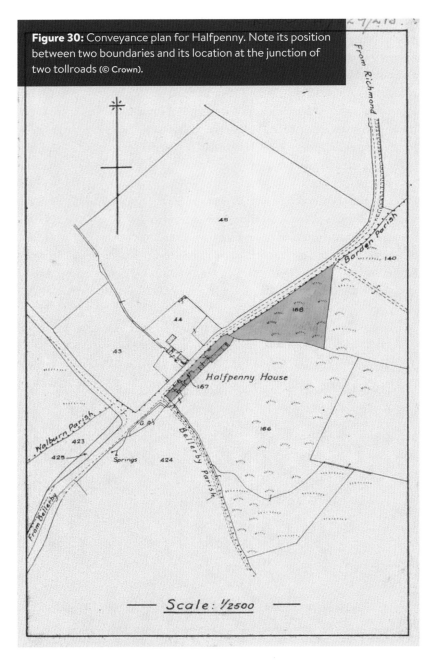

Figure 30: Conveyance plan for Halfpenny. Note its position between two boundaries and its location at the junction of two tollroads (© Crown).

Figure 31a: Halfpenny House in the 1920's
(Courtesy of Clive Torrens).

Figure 31b: Halfpenny House exterior today
(Jez Kalkowski, © Crown).

Figure 32a: The old Brewhouse at Halfpenny House with
detail showing the name plaque (Phil Abramson, © Crown).

Figure 32b: The stream that runs beneath the old Brewhouse
provided the water for the ale (Phil Abramson, © Crown).

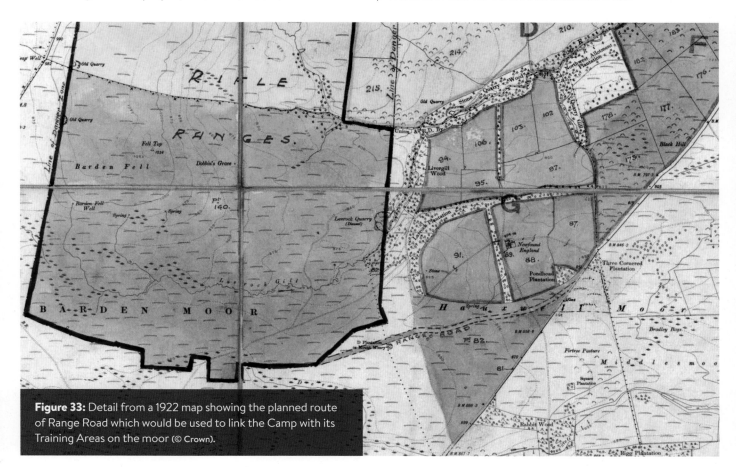

Figure 33: Detail from a 1922 map showing the planned route
of Range Road which would be used to link the Camp with its
Training Areas on the moor (© Crown).

Chapter 6
Historic Buildings on the Training Area

Historic Buildings on the Training Area

Given the army's propensity for destruction it is heartening to know that there are several historic buildings on the Training Area that have not only survived intact but are considered to be of national importance. Several books have been written describing the character and architecture of the historic buildings that are situated within Catterick's environs but this chapter, based on research carried out by Catterick Conservation Group members, looks at some of the particularly significant buildings that make up the Training Area portfolio.

Cordilleras Farm

The Farmstead

Three facts confronted former Conservation Group member Lieutenant Colonel Hugh Le Messurier when he first considered researching the history of Cordilleras and its position on Feldom Training Area. The first (which came as no surprise) was that Feldom is high (some 350m above sea level), windswept and remote – exactly the sort of inhospitable open ground that the army seems to favour in the training (or endurance testing!) of its troops.

The second fact was altogether less expected; that this bleak landscape contains a farmhouse named Cordilleras. Why would anyone choose to farm at such an altitude and why name your farm 'Cordilleras', a name which conjures up images of the warm South American plain rather that the cold, desolate beauty of a Yorkshire moor?

Last, but not least, is the most surprising fact of all: for all the privations imposed by the weather and its isolated position Cordilleras became an exemplar of farming success, built as one of the famed, technically-advanced model farms of the early 19th century *(Figure 1)*.

When the Hutton family began to develop their Marske Estate in the 18th century they chose to ignore the surrounding high moors, an omission which Arthur Young lamented in his 1770 tour of northern England noting that he had found *'the country all moors, and greatly improvable, but alas none undertaken.'* [1] He needn't have worried; only a few decades later John Hutton turned his attention and energies to the moorlands, beginning with the enclosure of Marske Moor in an Act of 1809 and building a new farm there, 550 feet above the village. His actions had largely been prompted by swiftly evolving events further afield. Corn prices doubled between 1790 and 1815, ushered in by a rapidly rising population and the onset of the Napoleonic Wars (1803–1815). In a bid to boost home production a wave of enclosures swept the county. Every acre of land needed to be used and cornfields expanded on to hitherto marginal land.

Given its elevated position Cordilleras was unlikely to have ever been an ordinary farm. At its helm was John Hutton known *'as a man of business, an acknowledged authority on philosophy and scientific agriculture'* who *'spread the gospel of new methods with enthusiasm throughout the district.'* [2] He was a friend of the Colling brothers and other noted breeders in the Darlington area and when they had a breakthrough with intensive in-breeding of Shorthorn cattle, Hutton was one of the first to breed early pedigree herds at his home farm in Marske. When the opportunity came to expand his experiments with the establishment of a new farm on the moors he seized it with enthusiasm.

The origins of the farm's unusual name seem to have been a combination of influences which included an admiration of mountains and the remarkable scientific publications and intrepid explorations of Alexander von Humboldt in Venezuela and the Andes. In the spirit of new discoveries Hutton settled on the name 'Cordilleras' for his own pioneering adventure and *'four South American volcanoes erupted on Marske Moor as names for his new fields'* [3] *(Figure 2)*.

1. Chapman, V., *Won from the Moor, North Country Farms of the Northern Fringe*, typescript, c.1970, p.8
2. Ibid
3. Chapman, V., *Won from the Moor, North Country Farms of the Northern Fringe*, typescript, c.1970

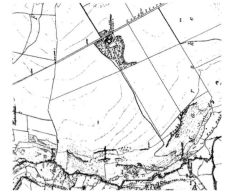

Figure 1: The 1st edition Ordnance Survey map of 1857 shows the remote location of Cordilleras Farm (Ref: 4OYNZ00SE).

Figure 2: 'A Plan of Cordilleras the property of Hutton (of Marske) Esq. Surveyed by Henry Rodham of Cooper House, 1824'. The South American influence extended beyond the farm's name to include the surrounding fields (Reproduced by permission of the North Yorkshire County Record Office. Ref: ZAZ(M)11).

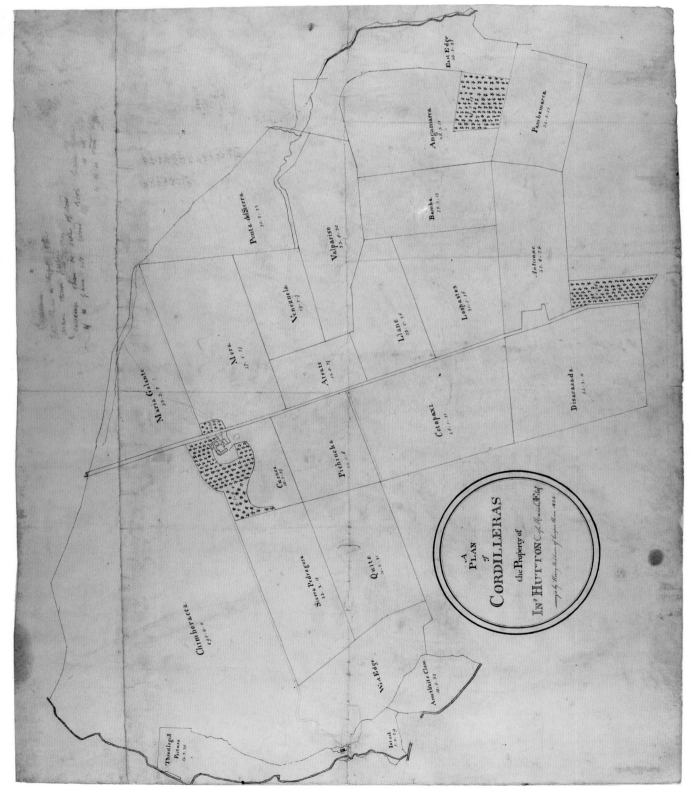

The years 1810 to 1812 was a period of intense activity and prepared the ground for the improvements in the years that followed. Road-making, walling, reclaiming the land and building the farmstead went side by side with large gangs of working men, women and children. Certainly it was back-breaking toil involving phenomenal amounts of labour and often working on steep inclines. Stone was quarried from the nearby fields for the foundations of farm buildings, roads had to be levelled and water holes had to be bored and pipes laid from 'Chimboracca' to bring water to the farmstead. Lime kilns were built and ploughs manufactured, initially of wood and then of iron, fired by the estate blacksmith. Something of the furious activity is captured in the following account:

'Shackholes and hollows were stuffed with quickens, sods, stones and soil and levelled… barren places were quarried down and covered with soil and manure, and earthfast stones broken up. Springs were intercepted, using bore rods for five springs in Lospastos bogs and bores and drains to seven feet deep in Venezuala bogs. Swangs and wet hollows were filled with sods and cobbles, and for the horses rolling Llano, the carpenter made horse clogs.'[4]

Their efforts were at last rewarded with the whole acreage of most fields fully cultivated by 1815. Even by today's standards it is hard to believe that at an elevation of 1,100 feet oats, rape, turnips and clover were grown and up to 100 Scottish and mixed herds wintered in addition to upwards of 600 sheep. Furthermore, in a bid to promote the farm's achievements Hutton staged agricultural shows, premium days and dinners at Cordilleras attracting competitors from miles around (Figure 3). History itself speaks of the farm's success. Before reverting to pasture, Cordilleras continued to enjoy several years of steady progress in spite of the agricultural slump which followed the end of the Napoleonic Wars.

Figure 3: Sale of farm stock at Cordilleras Farm, c.1930 (Courtesy of Mr & Mrs D Calvert).

The Farmhouse

Cordilleras Farmhouse was built between 1810-1813 by Hutton's own masons, carpenters and labourers using materials hewn from the surrounding landscape – the order and progress of building dictated by the rate of land reclamation. Vernacular in construction and design it still manages to infuse something of its name into the architecture with a Spanish-style main archway and tower.[5] First to be built was the house (inhabited from 1813) before other wings were added thus creating three complete foldyards. The buildings reflect the multitude of agricultural pursuits this exceptional farm was able to achieve. They included a horse-way, stabling, cartsheds, cowsheds, foddering houses and calf houses, pighouses, graneries, haylofts (one of which included a threshing machine), smith's shop and even a pigeon cote complete with cupola. Noteworthy features included a steaming house for potato feed preparation and a drying kiln, but the most unusual was the integral horse-way which was used for the threshing of corn, a feature which was extremely advanced for the period (Figure 4).[6]

Cordilleras today

Following John Hutton's death in 1841 the farm and lands continued to be used right up until, and even after, its purchase by the War Office in 1940 (Figures 5, 6, 7). The last tenants to live there, Mr. and Mrs. R. J. Lawson must be credited with extreme tolerance and stamina as for many years Feldom was used for live firing with 3-inch and 81mm mortar lines established near the farmhouse with the nearby Vickers gun lines necessitating the closure of the public Marske-Rake Gate road! Finally HQ Northumberland District requested that the Lawsons depart and the house fell victim to vandalism, the beautiful fixtures stolen or destroyed.

4. Ibid, p.11
5. The Spanish-style entranceway was noted by English Heritage when Cordilleras was Listed on 25 April 2005
6. Le Messurier, Lieut. Col. H.S., 'Cordilleras Farm' in *Catterick Training Centre*, publication issued by The Ministry of Defence and Conservation, 1990, p.11

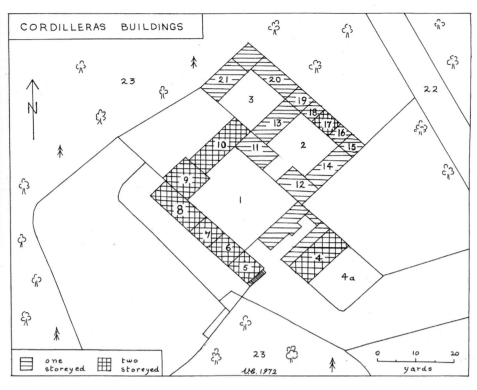

CORDILLERAS BUILDINGS

Figure 4 (left): Plan of Cordilleras Farm buildings, showing their change of use over the century between John Hutton's time and the Brown family's. The Brown family farmed at Cordilleras during the 1920s (From Le Messurier, H.S, 'Cordilleras Farm' in West Feldom , report by Catterick & Feldom Conservation Group, p. 33).

Figure 6a (top) & 6b (middle): The Tweddell family and friends relaxing in the front garden at Cordilleras Farmhouse, c.1930 (Courtesy of Mr & Mrs D Calvert).

CORDILLERAS BUILDINGS

	IN JOHN HUTTON'S TIME. c. 1824 (Hutton MSS and buildings)	IN HENRY BROWN'S BOYHOOD. c.1923 (recollections)
1, 2, 3	foldyard	foldyard, 2a midden steads
4, 4a	house and garden	house
5	3-horse stable and hay loft	calf house and hay loft
6	3-horse stable and hay loft	3-horse stable and hay loft
7	3-arched cart shed	back cart shed, wool store over
8	threshing barn	barn with wool store and granary over
9	4-arched hourse-way, granary over	cart shed and loft
10	barn and granary over	calf house and hay barn
11	? byre	byre
12	–	calf house
13	feeding sheds, cattle sheds	heifer house
14	? byre	byre
15	–	hay
16	2-horse stable	loose box for dales' pony
17	entrance arch, pigeon cote with cupola	entrance arch
18	2-horse stable	ducks
19	–	foal box
20	cattle shed, 4-arched	–
21	cattle shed, 4-arched	hog house (sheep under one-year-old)
22	Barningham Road (the spine road)	Cordilleras Road

Figure 5: The Tweddell family car outside Cordilleras Farmhouse, c.1930. The Tweddell family lived and farmed at Cordilleras during the 1930s (Courtesy of Mr & Mrs D Calvert).

Figure 7: Farmworkers outside farmyard entranceway, Cordilleras, c.1930 (Courtesy of Mr & Mrs D Calvert).

The surrounding landscape, which by now was operated as an open ranch, became overgrazed, choked by thistles and torn up by military vehicles.

Happily for Cordilleras its story is far from over. Since the 1970s numerous advances and improvements to the area have been made thanks to a joint partnership between various agencies including the Defence Infrastructure Organisation and English Heritage. Under their aegis the land ceased operating as an open ranch, heather moorlands were recovered and plantations established.
Efforts have also been made to restore the house to something of its former glory. While it is no longer a farm, Cordilleras today is far from being an empty shell and now serves as a base and headquarters for a variety of military units engaged in training…so long as it is not damage the fabric of the building *(Figures 8, 9)*.

Any fears that Cordilleras's position in the centre of an army Training Area has damaged its remarkable reputation will be assuaged by the knowledge that the farmstead's qualities still attract attention far and wide. In 1999 the published diaries of playwright Alan Bennett included an entry on Cordilleras where he mused on the farm as being an unexpected slice of South America hidden within the moors:

'Today the farm, with its echoes of the pampas, has been swallowed up by the Ministry of Defence's Training Area and so is now the playground of those upright and blameless young men recently corrupted by the shameless women of Catterick.'[7]

Fortunately subsequent official records afford Cordilleras a rather more dignified entry than an association with the alleged promiscuity of the locals!

In April 2005 Cordilleras Farmstead was awarded Grade II Listed Building status and credited with a lengthy entry in the records. The final paragraph sums up Cordilleras's importance in architectural history and it is possible to perhaps detect the inspector's wonder at its achievements:

'The planned farmstead is not only a very complete example of its kind dating from the first years of the nineteenth century, it is also one of the highest and most remote of the 'Model Farms' of the period, built where nothing stood before…it has an interesting history that reflects the fortunes of the country, and an awareness of international affairs.'[8]

Figure 8 (top): Cordilleras farmhouse today (Phil Abramson, © Crown).

Figure 9 (bottom): Entrance to foldyard with pigeon cote above (Phil Abramson, © Crown).

Figure 10a: Hipswell Hall, 1908
(Courtesy of Clive Torrens).

Figure 10b: Hipswell Hall today
(Phil Abramson, © Crown).

7. Bennett, A., *What I did in 1998*, Diaries, Vol. 21 No.2, 21 January 1999, pp 3-8
8. Building ID: 492360, www.britishlistedbuildings.co.uk
9. Page, W., (ed). *Victoria County History: A History of the County of York North Riding*, Volume 1, 1914, pp.310 – 313
10. See www.hipswellparish.org.uk The Churches of Hipswell Parish

Hipswell Hall

The crenellated parapet of Hipswell Hall *(Figure 10)* reminds us of the time when the lord of the manor was dominant here, long before the garrison town which now envelops it ever existed. The Hall, a Grade I listed building, can trace its origins back to the 15th century when it was a fortified manor house belonging to the Fulthorpe family. The 'Manor' of Hipswell, in which the hall is situated, is far older. Prior to the Conquest, Tor was the Saxon lord before he was replaced by Enisant Musard [9], a Norman tenant under Count Alan in Richmond. Although there is no obvious surviving evidence of this earlier occupation the remains of a chapel are recorded just a few hundred yards away from Hipswell Hall with documentary evidence suggesting a link back to the 13th century [10] *(Figure 11)*.

Hipswell first came into the Fulthorpe family hands in c.1318 when Roger de Fulthorpe took possession, providing the land on which his descendants would construct their family seat during the 15th century. It passed into the Wandesforde family's ownership when Anne and Cecily, the two daughters of 16th century owner John Fulthorpe, married the two Wandesforde brothers, Francis and Christopher. Quite how this family dynamic worked out is not made clear but it is sufficient to say that by the 1590s George Wandesforde, the grandson of Anne and Francis, was in residence and sufficiently prosperous to be able to afford to make improvements to his inheritance, adding the bold three-storey tower porch (complete with *'GW 1596'* inscribed above the doorway). Although substantial, the

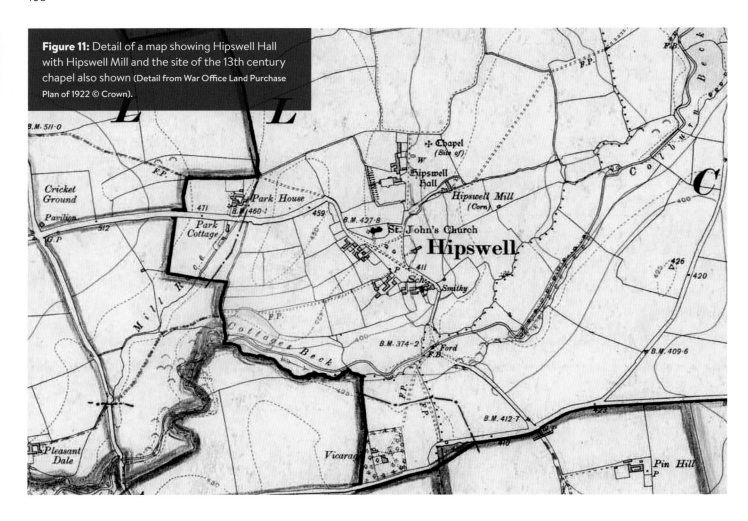

Figure 11: Detail of a map showing Hipswell Hall with Hipswell Mill and the site of the 13th century chapel also shown (Detail from War Office Land Purchase Plan of 1922 © Crown).

building seen today is far smaller than the one that George would have recognised. Originally consisting of a central block with two wings, enclosed by a moat and surrounded by terraced gardens, nowadays only one wing of the old manor house remains. Close by stood a mill and millhouse, the remains of which can still be seen. The nearby Hipswell Lodge, (shown on the 1922 Ordnance Survey map, *Figure 11)*, is said to have been modelled on Hipswell Hall and at least provides a good indication of the Hall's original layout.

Over time the hall's status diminished and whilst it remained in the Wandesforde family hands, from the 19th century onwards the building and its lands functioned more as a working farm than a high-status manor house. It is not documented where all the masonry from the original building disappeared to but certainly some of its stonework was incorporated into a new village church, St John's, which replaced an earlier dilapidated chapel. When the War Office came to make their purchase of Hipswell village in 1924 they found a manor house much diminished, and by now mainly serving as a hunting lodge for the Prior Wandesforde family. Its reduction however did not detract from its historic importance and it was regarded by English Heritage as *'a good example of its period,'* receiving Grade I listed status in 1969.

Downholme Hall

An entry in the Domesday Book records that Gospatric, a Saxon knight, held the 'Manor' of Downholme. Unusually Gospatric was also able to retain his possession of Downholme Manor for a couple of decades after Norman rule was in place and didn't cede it to Thomas de Richeburg until 1086. [11]

By the 14th century the Scrope family were in control of the manor and at some point during their early ownership Downholme Hall was constructed. Sadly, very little remains of their former seat today, the ruins of which are situated to the rear of the Bolton Arms in Downholme village. Archaeological investigations have at least extracted some clues as to the layout of the medieval hall. [12] For the most part the evidence uncovered has been fragmentary, but three barrel-vaulted chambers probably formed the basement of a fortified manor house *(Figure 12)*. Tantalising clues, such as the discovery of a small trefoil headed window at the eastern end, give an idea of what a grand building it must have once been – although this does now require a certain amount of imagination. A writer of a 1930s newspaper article cautioned any visitors to the hall's ruins:

11. Page, W., (ed).
    *Victoria County
    History: A History of
    the County of York
    North Riding Volume
    1*, 1914, pp.225-232

12. Turnbull, P.,
    *Downholme Hall Near
    Richmond, North
    Yorkshire: A Report
    for the Yorkshire
    Dales National Park*,
    November 1993

13. *Darlington and
    Stockton Times*, 31
    October 1936, p.10

14. See chapters 3
    and 5 for further
    information on the
    medieval village
    at Walburn

Figure 12 (left): Inside the barrel-vaulted cellar of Downholme Manor (Jez Kalkowski, © Crown).

Figure 13a (middle): Walburn Hall, 1906 (Courtesy of Clive Torrens).

Figure 13b (bottom): Walburn Hall today (Phil Abramson, © Crown).

'I discovered to my discomfort that the big room far from meriting the dignity of the mighty Scropes is comparable only with the Aegean stables. Even the cows have forsaken it.'[13]

Appearances are deceptive and although livestock may have forsaken the ruins, English Heritage officials are seemingly less fussy! Recognising the historic significance of the hall ruins they were designated a Grade II Listed Building in 1986.

Walburn Hall

Standing proud on the crook of the Richmond to Leyburn road Walburn Hall is one of the few fortified manor houses in the area that is still occupied and part of a working farm *(Figure 13a, 13b, 14)*. It is both architecturally and historically important and although much of the present-day structure dates mainly from the 15th and 16th centuries its foundation stretches back to the 12th century. At one time a medieval manor house stood in its place, and elements of this earlier building still survive as walls within the main building and the ruins of a chapel inside the grounds. [14]

Forgotten Facts

A Royal visitor

It is perhaps misleading to classify this as a forgotten fact for the tale of Mary Queen of Scots imprisonment at Walburn Hall is an association which has attracted a lot of attention over the years, most recently with a publication of a fictional account of her experiences.[16] Mary had arrived in the Dale when she was held prisoner at Bolton Castle by Lord Scrope. For a time she was held at Walburn Hall and the Elizabethan panelled room in which she was accommodated still survives today. Quite why she was transferred to Walburn during the period of her Yorkshire imprisonment is not certain but it may have been a decision her gaolers regretted when she made a bid for freedom by allegedly squeezing through a mullioned window to the road and waiting horse below.[17]

Figure 14: Walburn Hall, interior window.

From the outset the house had been built on a defensive plan, fulfilling the early obligations imposed on manors held under the Honour of Richmond to repel any invasions led by northern raiders. Just as today, the house was enclosed by crenellated walls and it is said, (with perhaps a touch of artistic license!), that if the villages heard of an impending raid:

'The men of Walburn would round up their cattle, drive them into the courtyard or an adjoining area also protected by the defensive wall, ram fast the outer gate, and then mount the platform in readiness to open a volley of arrows upon the foe.'[15]

In medieval times the manor belonged to the Bellerby family and then from the late 15th century to the Sidgwicks who built much of the present day manor house. Maybe it was a bid to recoup some of the costs for his family's home improvements, but Richard Sidgwick's decision to hike up the rents he imposed on his 16th century tenants was an action he was soon to regret. Resentment had been growing in the face of the unwelcome changes brought about by the Reformation and Sidgwick's ill-judged show of greed acted as touch paper to an already volatile situation. Angry masses swarmed upon Walburn Hall, and the lord was forced to witness parts of his property destroyed.

In 1618 the manor was sold to the Beckwith family and once again was a participant in historic events, when it was garrisoned against the King during the Civil War. The manor changed hands again in the 18th century when it was conveyed to John Hutton of Marske. The following century his descendent, Timothy, carried out restorations including the addition of battlements, defunct of their defensive purpose by this stage but something that the hall's earlier residents may have been grateful for (*Figures 15, 16*). It remained in the Hutton family's hands until the early years of the 20th century when the hall and its lands were purchased by the War Office.

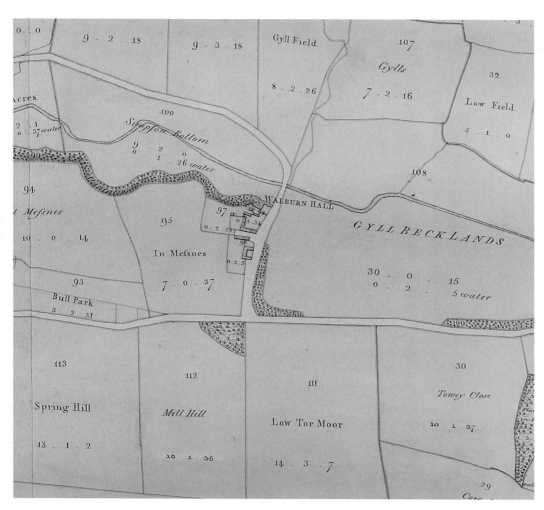

Figure 15 (left): Detail of Walburn Hall and the surrounding fields taken from: 'Plan of an Estate at Walburn belonging to T.Hutton, Esq 1821. T.Bradley, Richmond' (Reproduced by permission of the North Yorkshire County Record Office. Ref: ZAZ(M)13).

Figure 16 (bottom): Cartouche of the building in 1821 (Reproduced by permission of the North Yorkshire County Record Office).

The historic value of Walburn Hall was officially recognised when English Heritage inspectors visited the site in the 1960s. The Hall was designated a Grade I Listed Building and its courtyard wall Grade II in 1969. In October 2000 the historic significance of the medieval village, over which Walburn Hall had once lorded, was also recognised when it was designated a Scheduled Ancient Monument.

15. Wood, B. G., *Mary Stuart will never escape from Walburn Hall*, *Yorkshire Life Illustrated*, Vol. 11, 1957
16. Hayton, K., *A Queen Too Many*, 2010
17. Wood, B.G., *Mary Stuart will never escape from Walburn Hall*, *Yorkshire Life Illustrated*, Vol. 11, 1957

Chapter 7

Natural Partners?
The Army and the
Environment

Natural Partners?
The Army and the
Environment

Can the requirements of the army and the interests of the natural environment possibly co-exist? Modern military training, with its use of explosives, weaponry and heavy vehicles, conjures up an image which seems completely at odds with the forces of nature. Yet, as the following two reports by Conservation Group members Dr. Moira Owen and Major Tony Crease demonstrate, the very opposite is true. Catterick Training Area, far from being barren wasteland, instead teems with flora and fauna and even supports what is perhaps Britain's best protected, (given its position within an army base), Nature Reserve.

The Natural Environment of Catterick Training Area and Garrison [1]

It perhaps comes as a surprise to many people to find that military Training Areas are important for wildlife. The perception is that a military Training Area is likely to be a scene of desolation and the disturbance caused is likely to be damaging to the natural environment. The opposite is in fact true and the Defence Estate is recognised as being one of the most important land holdings for wildlife in the United Kingdom (UK). Catterick Training Area is a typical example. Within the Training Area there is internationally and nationally important heathland designated as a Special Area of Conservation (SAC), a Special Protection Area (SPA), Sites of Special Scientific Interest (SSSI), ancient woodlands and a variety of other habitats including grasslands, ponds and wetlands.

If the Catterick Training Area was a completely natural area it would be covered with woodland. In common with much of the UK, thousands of years of agricultural land management has largely removed the original woodland. However, relict areas of ancient woodland remain along the northern edge of Catterick Dry Training Area adjacent to the River Swale. The best examples are designated as part of the Lower Swaledale Woods and Grasslands SSSI. This includes High Spring Wood (*Figure 1*) and Side Bank Wood. In common with the rest of the Training Area, for health and safety reasons, (i.e. troops training with live ammunition and other military equipment), there is no public access, but these woodlands can be observed from the public highway running between Richmond and Reeth. Other examples include Ingsque Woods, Stainton Woods and woodland around Eddy's Bridge. There are also more modified woodlands further away from the River Swale running between Badger Beck and Sand Beck and between the Garrison and Richmond.

The most abundant canopy tree is ash, but there is also sycamore, alder, oak and birch. Previously, Wych elm was a locally frequent component of the canopy before the advent of Dutch elm disease. Many trees were lost but some were coppiced and subsequently recovered, with Wych elm now making a reasonable contribution to the sub-canopy in some places. Other elements of the understorey include hazel, holly, hawthorn and rowan.

Smaller pockets of ancient woodland [2] occur on Feldom. Associated with watercourses there are examples at Feldom Gill and Dalton Gill. The ancient woods usually occur on very steep ground, often with rock exposures and cliffs in situations where the tree cover has not been completely removed and trees have been able to persist out of reach of grazing animals. These habitats are amongst the most natural remaining in the UK. A feature of the crags is the existence of ancient individual trees including yew and rowan. Locations of notable veteran trees are currently being catalogued by Conservation Group members, particularly Tim Laurie and the Swaledale and Arkengarthdale Archaeology Group (SWAAG).

The flora of the ancient woodlands is varied and includes typical woodland plants such as dog's mercury, ramsons (also called wild garlic) and bluebell. There are also more rare species locally such as herb paris and goldilocks buttercup and of particular interest is the occurrence of the nationally rare prickly sedge.

Much of the woodland around the Training Area has been modified and includes areas where plantations have been created on open ground and blocks of conifers and non-native broadleaves have been planted on the ancient woodland sites. The woodlands have a long history of management. The area of woodland has increased in the late 20th century and more recently after an all-time low when woodlands in Swaledale were harvested for timber

and charcoal to fuel industrial and war-time activity. Planting of new areas commenced before the establishment of Catterick Training Area and can be credited to the previous estates that owned the land. These included conifer plantations with regular outlines such as at Gandale and Waitwith Bank plantations. More conifer plantations were created to provide a suitable environment for military training and to screen the Training Area. Recently the proportion of broadleaved trees has increased and opportunities have been taken to re-structure woodlands to give a more naturalistic effect.

A striking feature of the Garrison is its wooded character with mature plantations around the main barracks complexes, patches of semi-natural woodland and scrub near the Garrison becks, and amenity plantings and street trees. Wooded corridors link parts of the Training Area to the built environment of Catterick Garrison and beyond.

The wildlife supported by the woodlands is varied and includes mammals such as roe deer, badger and fox. Birds characteristic of upland woods such as pied flycatcher and redstart breed in the ancient woodlands and conifer specialists such as goldcrest and crossbill occur in the plantations. There is also a range of typical woodland birds, from tawny owls to tits, warblers and thrushes.

Little information is available on the invertebrate fauna of the woods but now-retired member of the Conservation Group Roy Crossley carried out a survey of the *Diptera* (flies) of High Spring and Far Spring Woods in 1993. A species list is available for soldier flies (*Stratiomyidae*), of which two are nationally notable, snipe flies (*Rhagionidae*) and of the 103 *Empidoidea* recorded, three are red data book and five notable. Hoverflies recorded include three woodland indicator species and two ancient woodland *Sciomyzidae* have been identified.

Areas of heathland have developed on the more acid soils. Upland heather moorland has a high nature conservation importance; the UK has international conservation obligations for this semi-natural habitat as so much of it occurs in this country compared to elsewhere. The western part of the Training Area which contains Bellerby Ranges is part of a large designated nature conservation site. Lovely Seat to Stainton Moor SSSI occupies the high ground between Swaledale and Wensleydale and is one of the best examples showing the gradation between blanket bog on

1. Report prepared by Dr Moira Owen, Natural Environment Advisor. Defence Infrastructure Organisation
2. Ancient woodland site is defined as having supported a continuous woodland cover since 1600 or earlier

deep peat in the west to dry heathland on Stainton Moor. It is also part of the large North Pennine Moors SAC and SPA. This is of importance for a range of upland habitats including blanket bog, heathland, juniper scrub and for breeding birds merlin, peregrine and golden plover *(Figure 2)*.

Much of the rest of the Training Area is effectively the moorland fringe, parts of which have a heathland character. Agricultural policies after WWII were designed to increase food production so sheep numbers were high and resulted in the loss of heather. Recent policies have reversed this trend and many of the tenant farmers are now in environmental stewardship schemes which aim to restore heather by reducing livestock numbers. Although, historically, grazing levels may have been higher than the ideal, in general, use of the land for military training has protected it from much of the agricultural intensification that has gone on elsewhere in the British countryside. The Training Area today is now a mosaic of bog, heathland and large areas of semi-natural grassland. Typical plants found are heather, cross-leaved heath, purple moor-grass, mat-grass, bent-grasses, fescues, rushes, bracken, tormentil and heath bedstraw *(Figure 3)*.

The Dry Training Area grassland is mostly neutral to acid and not particularly species-rich. Because enclosed fields around farmsteads are farmed more intensively and are mainly agriculturally improved permanent pastures and fields cut for silage, wild flower-rich meadows are now one of the rarest habitats in the UK. However, examples occur on Feldom and include limestone grassland around the crags and a small number of hay meadows. A more surprising feature of nature conservation importance is the sparse vegetation associated with mining spoil. Given the grand name of "Calaminarian Grassland" it contains specialised flowering and lower plants that can tolerate the high lead and zinc levels found in mining spoil such as mountain pansy and alpine penny-cress. Mining spoil is scattered across Bellerby Ranges and Feldom, but is more plentiful further west and north in the Dales.

The extensive grasslands are important for ground nesting birds. There are curlews, lapwings, oystercatchers, snipe, skylarks, meadow pipits and grey partridges. Catterick also has a small and vulnerable population of black grouse *(Figure 4)*, found at the most easterly extent of the species current range. A feature of the Dry Training Area is the extensive covering of gorse which is a colourful spectacle in spring and supports other bird species of conservation concern such as linnets and yellowhammers.

Figure 2: Golden plover chick (Foxglove Covert, © Crown).

Figure 3 (left): A variety of habitats on the training area looking towards Wathgill Camp (Jo Haskett, Landmarc Support Services Ltd).

Figure 5 (below): Typical uplands fast-flowing stream (Jo Haskett, Landmarc Support Services Ltd).

Water is another important aspect of the Training Area. Due to the low intensity of agriculture, water quality is high and there are numerous gills and becks forming part of the catchment of the River Swale *(Figure 5)*. The flora and fauna are typical of fast-flowing upland streams and there are records for native crayfish and otter. Water draining from the Dry Training Area feeds streams running through the Garrison and here there is more adjacent woodland. There are dozens of ponds and 42 locations have been surveyed in detail. Many have been artificially dug for a variety of purposes including mining ponds, fish ponds, duck ponds, fire ponds and more recently some have been created for nature conservation objectives such as at Foxglove Covert. Species of conservation interest known to be present include the mud snail *Omphiscola glabra*, the lesser water boatman *Sigara limitata*, great crested newts and several rare water beetles. Other amphibians including toads, frogs and several newt species are also found.

Figure 4: *Tetrao tetrix* – Black grouse. The black cock is often seen on the training area (© Crown).

Figure 6: Green hairstreak
butterfly.

There are smaller-scale but often species-rich semi-natural wetland habitats across the estate. Small-scale mires or flushes support many species including rushes, sedges, mosses and a variety of flowering plants such as marsh-orchids, marsh valerian and marsh bedstraw. They are an important source of invertebrate food for the ground nesting birds on the estate. Of particular importance are the localised petrifying springs with tufa deposits on Bellerby ranges.

Some of the fauna are not confined to particular habitats: these include mobile species such as butterflies. Although there are exceptions, for example there is a substantial population of the heathland specialist green hairstreak butterfly on Bellerby ranges, butterflies and moths can be found across the estate. Over much of the British Countryside once common

butterflies have declined but Catterick Conservation Group members have continued to record up to 24 species across the Training Area *(Figure 6)*.

There are many generalist species of birds scattered across the Training Area, found in woodlands or utilising hedgerows and scrub in the more open habitats. These include species of conservation concern such as song thrush, dunnock and various tits and finches. Field boundaries vary between hedgerows on the low ground around the Garrison and walls on the moorland at Bellerby and Feldom.

What can be seen from this short account is that Catterick Training Area has an exceptional biodiversity and that management of the land for military training has safeguarded flora and fauna that has declined elsewhere in the wider countryside.

Foxglove Covert Local Nature Reserve [3]

Foxglove Covert Local Nature Reserve started life as a small Conservation Area to the rear of Cambrai Lines. During the IRA campaign in the early 1970s a tall security fence was installed around the barracks to prevent any incursion, and thereafter the area now within the reserve became a landlocked wilderness with no access. For 20 years it lay fallow until the Conservation Area was initiated in 1992 by which time the site had become a heavily overgrown area of willow carr and wet pools.

In September that year work began to improve and develop the habitat and 28 acres were granted to The Royal Scots Dragoon Guards (SCOTS DG) who were the resident Royal Armoured Corps Training Regiment (RACTR) at the time. A decision had been taken as part of the 'Options for Change' initiative to move the Training Regiment to Bovington and as a result both SCOTS DG and RACTR personnel worked on the area for several months pending re-roling and transfer of personnel to Dorset (Figure 7).

Bird ringing activities took place from the very early days and a grant from Regimental Funds of £300 produced a garden shed which was very quickly added to as the site headquarters (Figure 8). On an annual rotational basis habitat management continued and winter projects such as beck and heathland clearance, willow coppicing and pollarding, the creation of ponds and the lake, the construction of paths and a road, took place. The weir and slipway at the lake were repaired and the lake above the dam, which was heavily silted and had trees growing in it, was cleared out. It was later learned that the dam had been built by trawlermen from Lowestoft and Great Yarmouth who had been seconded to Catterick en masse in 1915. At the outbreak of WWI they had been forbidden from putting to sea because of German U-boat activity off East Anglia and instead they had been brought to Catterick to facilitate water supply, that essential component necessary to allow the construction of billets for 40,000 servicemen. All timber supplies had gone to the war effort and sufficient water for a large, entirely concrete urbanisation, was vital to the building programme in the early days of the Garrison. That same dam continues to hold water over a century later, and the metal helical drainage wheels still continue to function.

The following seven years saw continual change and constant improvement to the habitat mosaic. A damaged SCOTS DG Regimental Recruiting Caravan was repaired and brought on site and this was used as the Headquarters and ringing room for over five years. Then the guardroom portacabin from Megiddo Lines was brought in and that served as the main hub for a further three years.

3.   Report prepared by Major Tony Crease

Figure 7 (above): Early days of Foxglove Covert; assistance bringing in the recruiting caravan (Foxglove Covert, © Crown).

Figure 8 (right): The original bird ringing shed (Foxglove Covert, © Crown).

Figure 9 (above):
Construction of the
field centre (Foxglove
Covert, © Crown).

Figure 10 (left):
Field Marshall Sir John
Chapple and Major
Tony Crease outside
the newly opened
field centre (Foxglove
Covert, © Crown).

Figure 11 (left): The scrapes during their construction (Foxglove Covert, © Crown).

Figure 12 (below): The scrapes after construction (Jo Haskett, Landmarc Support Services Ltd).

As the Conservation and Ringing Areas improved and new habitats were exposed it became clear that the area had more to offer than initially thought. As a result, in 1999, a process was begun to turn the site into the first Local Nature Reserve in Richmondshire and that was exactly what happened. In conjunction with English Nature (now Natural England) and Richmondshire District Council, Local Nature Reserve status on MOD land was granted on 6th April 2001. Foxglove was also the first Local Nature Reserve to be designated on MOD land anywhere in the country.

The new reserve became increasingly popular and it was soon obvious that the existing spartan facilities could not cope with the number of visitors. A Management Group was formed and a decision taken in 2000 to seek adequate funding for an Activity and Education Centre – later to become known as the Field Centre – which it was estimated would cost £300k. With significant assistance from the Works Service Manager at HQ Catterick Garrison plans were drawn up and letters were sent out seeking funding that ultimately accrued the very handsome sum of £350k leaving some wriggle room for better and additional interpretation facilities. The centre was built and opened officially, to great acclaim, by Field Marshal Sir John Chapple on 30th October 2002 *(Figures 9, 10)*.

The Field Centre became the platform for many further successes and there followed a period of 10 very productive years. A single warden was employed initially and this was later extended to two Reserve Managers. The reserve itself was increased in size on at least two occasions with the wetland on the moor and then Range Plantation being added. Habitat quality continued to improve, inappropriate trees were removed and replaced in their hundreds, and a well-managed natural area, interspersed with suitably maintained pathways, made the reserve extremely popular with young and old, dedicated naturalists and casual visitors, military and civilian personnel from the local community, and many families on visits to the Dales area generally *(Figures 11-14)*. High profile visitors included none other than The Prince of Wales, the Head of Natural England, William Hague MP, Vice Admiral Tim Lawrence, and other well-known national figures with a natural history background.

In order to encourage further support from the MOD, ownership of the Field Centre by the Trust was relinquished in 2007 and responsibility for maintenance and statutory works, the access road and many of the footpaths was assumed by the MOD contractor, Landmarc Support Services Ltd. This principle was further followed in March 2010 when Natural England offered the opportunity to enter into a 10 year Higher Level Stewardship environmental agreement which delivered additional funding and enhanced site maintenance opportunities. With this agreement came a £400,000 capital grant payment, which included major projects like the easy access, the lake extension, the outdoor classroom and the moorland trail *(Figure 15)*.

Foxglove is an amazing Catterick Garrison facility and a remarkable mosaic of species-rich habitats. Over 2440 different species have been recorded on the reserve. It has twice won the coveted MOD Sanctuary Award and is at the very forefront of conservation and environmental activity in and around Richmondshire. It is a Centre of Excellence in the science of bird ringing with over 100,000 birds processed on the site and 40,000 seabirds processed on the annual expeditions mounted to the Air Weapons and Naval Bombardment Range at Cape Wrath. Over half a million people have visited the reserve and more than

20,000 school children have benefited from educational visits. Close to a million people have viewed the website and two television programmes have been recorded reflecting the diversity of the wildlife to be found there. Two hundred bird ringers have attended courses and over 100 beekeepers are among 1500 other local organisations to have used the facilities regularly in recent years. The indoor bee observation hive is one of very few in the country.

The reserve is an outstanding example of the military engaging with the local community and the results are evident and tangible.

Figure 14 (left):
View of the
completed
wetlands hide
(Foxglove Covert,
© Crown).

Figure 15 (below):
The outdoor
classroom at
Foxglove Covert
(Foxglove Covert,
© Crown).

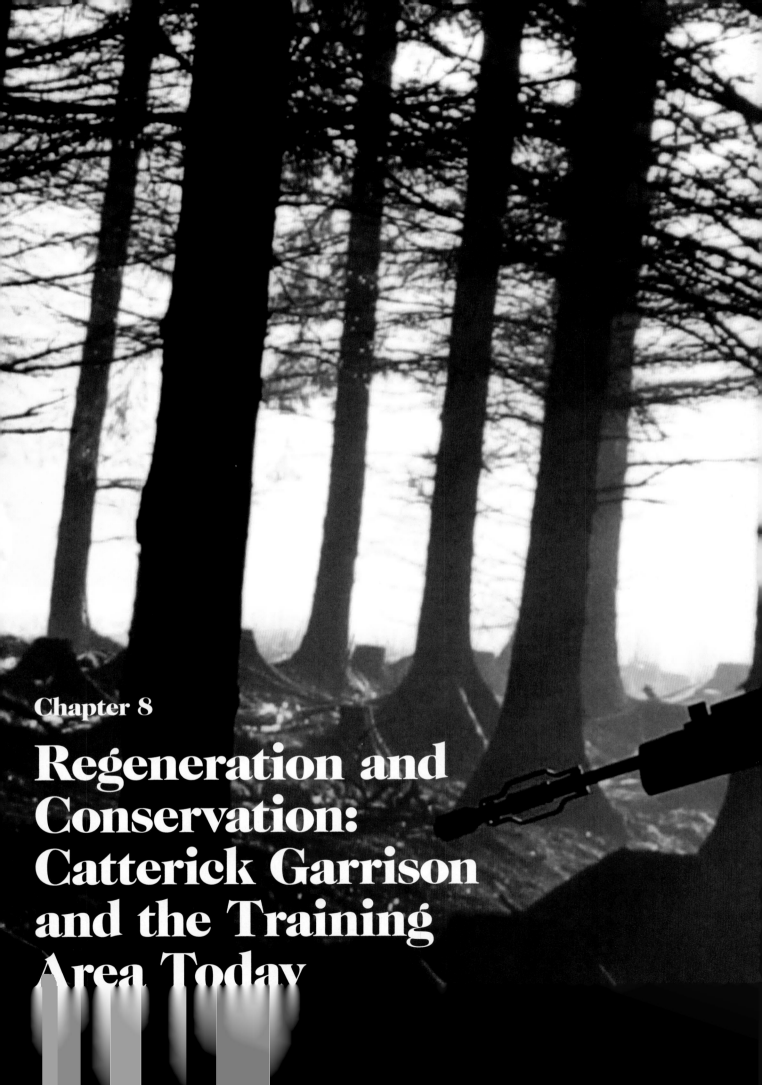

Chapter 8

Regeneration and Conservation: Catterick Garrison and the Training Area Today

Regeneration and Conservation: Catterick Garrison and the Training Area Today

The Garrison: A Regeneration Story

When Field Marshall Viscount Montgomery visited Catterick in April 1947 he remarked *"This isn't a Camp, it's a town."* His words were prophetic for on January 1st 1973 Catterick Camp officially changed its name to Catterick Garrison. And whilst not attaining the ranking of a town, as proclaimed by the Field Marshall, the name change removed the temporary status implied by the word 'Camp' and provided a permanent status which also asserted the military character of the site.

When the announcement came it served to justify the continuing work that had taken place in the years which followed WWII to improve the Camp's facilities. The problem, as contemporary planners explained, was that the architectural development of the Camp had been distorted by the emergency requirements of two world wars. Inevitably the wars had left a legacy of financial constraints but it did not prevent the planners from seeing a bright future for Catterick Garrison:

'Although the new Catterick must necessarily remain predominantly a military town, those responsible for its development can see no reason why it should not be well laid out and attractive. We aim to create a station, which the soldier will enjoy and look back on with pleasure, and a military centre which may be a source of pride both to the army and to the North of England.'[1]

Cambrai and Alma Barracks [2] were completed in 1963, swiftly followed by Somme Barracks in 1964 and Harden Barracks in 1967. A new hospital, named the Duchess of Kent Military Hospital, was opened in 1974, replacing the 200-bed hospital built during WWI.

At the same time a number of royal visits and inspections by senior military staff demonstrated Catterick's growing importance, and it was also recognised that integration with, and support from, the wider community was needed. Relationships were cemented through the 'civilianisation' of the Garrison staff whereby many positions, both clerical and manual, which had formerly been filled by soldiers, were transferred to civilians. The resulting growth in employment led to the construction of more housing estates, involving the local authority in the fields of housing, employment and welfare. Landholdings were increased in 1994 when the site of RAF Catterick was handed over to the army who promptly renamed it Marne Barracks *(Figure 1)*.

In the midst of this spirit of regeneration there were some casualties. The Officers' Club and St. Oswald's Garrison Church were both demolished between 1967 and 1969, with the demolition of the latter reportedly being so speedy that worshippers arriving to attend a Sunday morning service found that their church had gone! *(Figure 2)*. A further loss was the closure of the Camp railway service. On 26th October 1964, the last passenger train drew out of Catterick Camp station, and five years later, on 8th December, the last train left the Camp, and the station closed. In more recent times the General Post Office *(Figure 3)* was pulled down in 2003 to make way for a supermarket.

Catterick Garrison is currently undergoing a huge programme of expansion and upgrading of its facilities. A 'Long Term Development Plan' has been prepared which puts Catterick firmly on the map as one of the largest and most up-to-date garrisons in Europe.

1. Cole, Lt. Col. Howard N., *The Story of Catterick Camp*, The Forces Press, Aldershot, 1972, p.58
2. Alma was the first battle of the Crimea War and is the only barracks built in Catterick at that time to bear a name of a battle prior to the 1914-18 war

Figure 1: Oran House on Marne Barracks was built in the 1830s and is a Grade II Listed Building. It was used as Officers' accommodation until the mid 1990s (Phil Abramson, © Crown).

Figure 2 (left): St Oswald's Church, Catterick Garrison (Catterick Garrison HQ collection).

Figure 3 (above): Post Office building shortly before demolition (Phil Abramson, © Crown).

The Training Area: A Conservation Story

Alongside the residential and commercial developments on the Garrison, action was also taking place to improve the terrain on which (the by now comfortably accommodated) troops could train. In tandem with these advances was a growing awareness of the historical and ecological importance of the MOD Estate.

Firstly, it is worth looking at how the Training Area developed in the years following the two World Wars. In the 1920s infantry rifle skills, so recently used on the battlefields, were seen as being of paramount importance, leading to the construction of three gallery ranges at Deerpark, Whipperdale and Herontree, to replace those on Barden Moor. By the 1960s technology had advanced considerably and the first electric target range was opened at Whitfell in 1968 with the range at Deerpark following suit in 1970 *(Figures 4)*.

Modern training facilities needed a modern training centre from which to operate, and in 1959 the first Commandant of Catterick Training Centre, Brigadier E. D. Good was appointed and granted an office at the Headquarters of the Garrison *(Figures 5a, 5b)*. Ten years later it was decreed that Catterick Training Centre was to become an Infantry Skill at Arms Camp (ISAAC). The extent of this task made it apparent that Brigadier Good's successor, Lieutenant Colonel Hugh le Messurier, would require a separate, suitable base from which to operate. In 1971 Command was set up at Bellerby Camp but with plans already in place to build a new camp at Wathgill *(Figure 6a, 6b)*. The new camp was opened in 1982 with Bellerby Camp closing a year later.

Figure 4: Preparing for operations on the Heavy Machine Gun (WO1 RSM Bill Bean © Crown).

Figure 5a (top left): Catterick Garrison HQ during WWII (Catterick Garrison HQ collection).

Figure 6a (bottom left): The original Wathgill Camp, 1937 (Courtesy of Clive Torrens).

Figure 5b (top right): A recent photograph of Catterick Garrison HQ – nothing has changed except the time on the clock! (Phil Abramson, © Crown).

Figure 6b (bottom right): Wathgill Camp today (Jez Kalkowski, © Crown).

By this stage the Training Area at Catterick was able
to offer an impressive range of troop training facilities
in a variety of conditions from open moorland to dense
woodland *(Figures 7, 8)*. One of the more unusual sites
was used for practising warfare drills and skills in a replica
urban environment – a need which had arisen in the
1970s following operations in Northern Ireland. Initially
negotiations were made with Darlington Town Council
to allow soldiers to be deployed onto the town's streets. As
requirements grew, a decision was taken to convert 18
married quarter buildings at the Whinny Hill Estate into
a 'Fighting in Built Up Areas' or FIBUA complex (the
word 'fighting' was changed in 1999 to 'Operations' and
FIBUAs became OBUAs) *(Figures 9, 10)*. The houses were
augmented with a custom made high-rise building to give
troops the experience of defending and assaulting blocks
of flats, a tunnel system and a 'Molotov Cocktail' facility
(Figures 11). Latterly closed circuit television for post-
exercise debriefings and a battle-simulation audio system
were added. Its provision of highly realistic and imaginative
facilities mean that it is used not only by the army but also
by the police, fire brigade and foreign troops.

As the years passed Catterick's importance continued to

Figure 9 (below): Officers' quarters at Whinny Hill
(Catterick Garrison HQ collection).

Figure 7 (above):
The Mortar Platoon
making best use of a
range day (WO1 RSM
Bill Bean © Crown).

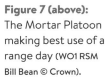

Figure 8 (above): Dry firing on the
Training Area (Jez Kalkowski, © Crown).

Figure 10 (left): Aerial view of the Whinny
Hill OBUA (Operations in Built-Up Areas)
complex (© Crown).

Figure 11: Using the Molotov Cocktail area at Whinny Hill OBUA (Jez Kalkowski, © Crown).

into 12 Training Areas and so in 1999 yet another title (and acronym!) was bestowed upon the command at Wathgill Camp when it became the principal Army Training Estate in the North East (ATE NE). Along with its new title came a greater workload and additional responsibility was assumed for two other training areas at Ripon and Strensall.

By 2008 financial constraints led to yet another round of restructuring of the army training facilities (and inevitably another title). The original 12 ATEs were reduced to nine Defence Training Estates (DTEs). The ATEs of the North East and the North West were merged to form DTE North based at Wathgilll Camp, representing a huge and impressive area of responsibility best summed up by former Range Officer Major (Retd) Tim Helps in 2012:

"Thus from the HQ at Wathgill Camp, which a dozen years ago only had to be concerned with Catterick, Feldom and Battle Hill, the Commander – a serving Lt Col – is responsible for Catterick, Warcop and Otterburn and all their outstations. Totalling some 150,000 acres spread over the North of England coast to coast, Humber to the Tweed – Lord Baden-Powell would have been impressed."

grow. With responsibility for providing a training area for the largest garrison in the United Kingdom, the Catterick Training Area was re-designated an Army Field Training Centre (AFTC) in 1994. Under the stewardship of the AFTC Commandant, Lieutenant Colonel Morris Felton, a Conservation Project Officer was appointed. One of the key aims behind the appointment was to help re-establish three disappearing species – the red squirrel, the otter and the black grouse – onto the Training Areas. This strategy was

proof (as the newly appointed officer was to say) that the military was a credible conservation force 'not just about blowing the countryside up, we do have a positive conservation and management strategy'[3] *(Figure 12)*.

In the meantime the Warminster-based Headquarters for the Army Training Estates were busy deciding how best to manage their countrywide landholdings (which today amount to some 240,000 hectares). The decision was made to restructure the country

3. Conservation Project Officer Max Garrety, Yorkshire Post, 9 August,1996
4. List taken from 'Military Training', Ministry of Defence and Conservation Catterick Training Centre, unpublished booklet, 1990

Forgotten Facts

Wathgill Camp wins architectural accolade

In 1978 the plans for the soon-to-be constructed Wathgill Camp were selected for their architectural merit and hung in the Royal Academy's Summer Exhibition. The successful design subsequently went on to become the blueprint for the construction of future bases. Proving that fit for purpose needn't mean an eyesore, special efforts were made to make sure that it blended in with the surrounding countryside by using re-claimed Yorkshire stone and employing clever landscaping techniques.

A 'nuclear' explosion at Scotton village

The decision to employ the sophisticated sound system, now used to great effect at the OBUA training facility, came about in a rather explosive manner – and at the cost of several Scotton villagers' nerves! Over the years of being neighbours to an active military Training Area, residents of the surrounding villages have adopted an admirable degree of stoicism at the sometimes loud and unpredictable nature of training. However the fear that they had just witnessed a 'nuclear' explosion one October morning in 1999 shook even the calmest residents into a state of panic.

The culprits were not British troops but the Third Belgian Parachute Battalion who had been using the OBUA training facility. Their brief had included the simulation of a number of bangs and a 'mock-nuclear explosion'. So realistic was the effect generated by the pyrotechnics they had used that the sky was reportedly filled by a huge mushroom cloud, window panes shattered in nearby buildings, the accompanying bang heard a mile away and even an army spokesperson, exhibiting a master class of practised understatement, was forced to admit that 'it was a bit louder than expected.'[5] In the midst of dealing with the understandable calls for compensation, training area staff realised that a more user and neighbour friendly sound system had to be found. Trials began and by the following year the new sound system (similar to those used at pop concerts) was in place. Thanks to that alarming autumn morning, training troops are furnished with realistic battle sounds including artillery bombardment, air strikes, armoured movement and small arms fire. As good action scenes need a good director it should come as no surprise to learn that Steven Speilberg has a mention here – the sound track from 'Saving Private Ryan' is reportedly one of the more popular high-intensity battle tracks used![6]

Conservation developments

At about the same time that plans were afoot to create a new base at Wathgill, thoughts also turned to the conservation responsibilities of those managing the Training Areas. As has been demonstrated in the previous chapters on ecology and archaeology, an unintended, but fortunate, consequence of military training over the years has been the preservation of flora and fauna that have disappeared or are 'at risk' in other areas of the country. Additionally, significant sites of archaeological and historic interest had also survived. Since the 1970s an interest in conservation had been growing within army circles and in 1976, under an initiative driven by Surrey-based Colonel Norman Claydon, Conservation Groups began to be set up in army training areas. In response to this initiative the 'Catterick and Feldom Conservation Group' (later Catterick Training Area Conservation Group) was formed in 1978 under Lieutenant Colonel Hugh Le Messurier. From its early days the membership has grown so that the Group can now boast an impressive list of military and civilian members. Disciplines covered include, Archaeology, Botany, Ecology Entomology, Forestry, Geology and Ornithology. Expert bodies are represented from the Natural England, Yorkshire Dales National Park, Yorkshire Wildlife Trust, Yorkshire Naturalists Union, RSPB and Richmondshire District Council.[4]

This pool of expertise has meant that the flora and fauna of the Training Area could be recorded, new species identified and those at risk earmarked for attention, in some cases through the creation of new wildlife habitats. The Catterick Wetland Projects of 1983-89 oversaw the creation of six ponds and one lake, providing a

5.   The Northern Echo, 15 October, 1999
6.   Helps, T., How Saving Private Ryan Makes OBUA Training a Blast, In the Field, 2002.
7.   Helps, T., Catterick – Creating a Multi-Headed Hydra, In the Field, Autumn 1999, p.2
8.   Helps, T., Sanctuary, 1999

Figure 13 (right): A modest opinion of the outcome of two projects in the minutes of the Conservation and Feldom Conservation Group in 1992! (Courtesy of Tim Helps).

Figure 12 (below): Public Information leaflet on Catterick Training Area neatly outlining the Army's duel responsibilities of training soldiers whilst protecting the environment (© Crown).

CATTERICK and FELDOM CONSERVATION GROUP

MINUTES OF THE AUGUST '92 MEETING, BATTLE HILL,

21 August 1992.

CONSERVATION MEGA-SUCCESS
REGENERATION OF HEATHER MOORLAND   SUPERB NEW POND - STURDY SPRING, FELDOM

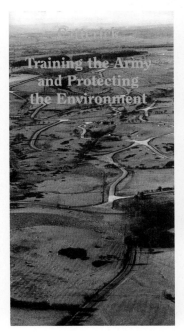

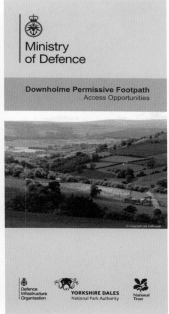

haven for wildlife including herons, coots, oystercatchers, mallards, teal and frogs (or at least those lucky enough to evade some of the above!). Their achievements led to the Group being given the 'Silver Otter Award', a prestigious MOD Conservation prize, in 1992. In the same year the Group was also credited with the completion of a 92,000 tree planting scheme and 380 hectares of heather conservation (*Figure 13*).

As Conservation Groups made their presence known within the MOD regions, those in charge of army land management began to realise what benefits they could bring. Presenting a rare opportunity for a civilian and military partnership they were able to support a sustainable and conservation-aware policy with the twin goals of meeting the army's training needs and the protection of a precious historic and natural environment. It meant that while the land continued to be used by troops and vehicles for training purposes the input provided by conservation groups helped, where possible, to minimise the potentially damaging effects of their activities. In 1997 a manoeuvre area of more than 50 square kilometres was created which allowed soldiers to carry out their training without their tracked vehicles damaging the environment (*Figures 14*). Defence Estates Forestry Department was then tasked in

turn to create a woodland shield with which to blend the project into the surroundings, planting some 73,000 trees between 1996 and 1998.[7]

Damage caused by past activities has also received attention. The dawn of the new millennium saw the completion of a Conservation Group project to reinstate some of the 18th and 19th century stone walling on Feldom Moor. The walling, a testimony to ancient building skills, represented hours of back-breaking work using teams of horses and carts to transport the stone from the nearby quarries. In the 1940s, when troops began to use the area to practise, conservation issues had been low on the list of priorities and little thought was given to the painstaking hours of labour that the troops were driving roughshod over. An opportunity presented itself in the late 1990s to at least begin to right an earlier wrong. Two 'Master Wallers' were employed and between October 1997 and April 1998 two thousand metres of walling were repaired (*Figures 15a, 15b*).[8]

A couple of years later the ugly scars resulting from army training exercises and building developments were the incentives for the Barden Fell Wetlands Project. The Fell, which peaks at 1,034 feet, had been the high point towards which cavalry charges were made in the 1920s but had

Figure 14: Aerial view of the manoeuvre area created in 1997. The aim was to limit damage to the environment caused by tracked vehicles, such as that shown in the inset (© Crown).

suffered considerably once mechanisation had displaced horses. Throughout WWII the Fell was used as a tank training area which carved up its grassland cover. War ending brought no respite for the Fell as it became part of the Training Area designated for tracked vehicles to practise cross-country driving. Matters were compounded with the flat top of the Fell proving a useful depository for building rubble from the adjacent Garrison. This had, in turn, been put to use by creating graded obstacles for armoured vehicles to drive over. The area was fast becoming an eyesore of track-churned muddy puddles and building detritus.

Out of these unpromising ingredients the inspiration for a rescue plan came about. Past observations had taught that if left undisturbed the pools created by vehicle tracks soon attracted plant life and aquatic insects. In 2000 the idea of creating a 'Conservation Crater' was born and, using redundant building rubble to create a 731 metre-wide circular bund, contractor William Metcalfe constructed a sequence of ponds. More than a decade later proof of the regenerative power of nature means that barely a scar remains of the former massive disturbance by man and machinery to the landscape. Frogs, newts, lizards and all manner of water birds now seek sanctuary within the crater.

The site has since been designated as a conservation area and is now out of bounds for military training *(Figures 16a, 16b)*.

Over the years the activities and achievements of the countrywide MOD Conservation Groups have led the Defence Infrastructure Organisation to formerly recognise their significance. In 2005 a review of Conservation Group Activities across the UK MOD Estates was undertaken. It acknowledged that as one of the largest landowners in the country the MOD has a major role to play in conservation and that the Conservation Groups, with their expert local knowledge, were an integral part of its conservation strategy. Since its inaugural meeting in January 1978 members of the Catterick Training Area Conservation Group have supported the MOD in fulfilling this aim. A fitting summary of its importance is simply put in the introduction of 2001 user guide to the Army Training Estate, North East. The words, although written more than a decade ago, are as true today as they were then... and will be in the future:

It can be seen from the above summary what an extremely important and precious place the ATE NE is. It is in everybody's interest to care for and preserve it. If we do not conserve it we will lose it.

Figure 15a (left): Repairing stone walling on Feldom Moor (Courtesy of Tim Helps).

Figure 15b (below): Repaired stone walling on Feldom Moor (Jo Haskett, Landmarc Support Services Ltd).

Forgotten Facts

This is a story without an end!

This book has presented an edited and condensed account of the research and fieldwork that the Catterick Conservation Group has carried out over the years, and hopefully shows how much it has managed to accomplish during its relatively short lifespan. Limitless potential exists for future research and discoveries and it is hoped that the book will act as an incentive to those who care about our historic and natural environment to add facts that have been omitted or forgotten and, in so doing, contribute towards the successes of the future.

Figure 16a (bottom of page): Barden fell Wetlands Project; creation of the crater (Courtesy of Tim Helps).

Figure 16b (below): Barden Fell Wetlands Project in 2007; a diverse natural habitat (Courtesy of Tim Helps).

Endpiece

Established in 1978, the Catterick Conservation Group has been at the forefront in championing the interests of the historic and natural environment on the Training Area. It still thrives and its members represent a range of conservation interests that could fill the pages of a university prospectus!

Lieutenant Colonel Le Messurier, Lieutenant Colonel Wade and Lieutenant Colonel Felton were instrumental in steering the group through its early years. Members of the group who have contributed to this book have been mentioned in the acknowledgements, but the commitment of those who have been part of the group over the years is also greatly appreciated. It is impossible to mention them all by name but without such stalwarts as Major (Retd) Tim Helps and Major (Retd) David Oldham where else would the birds and butterflies of the Training Area get such fulsome praise and attention and with Roy Crossley the flies of the Training Area had a true friend. The educational work reported by the staff of Foxglove Covert provides a link between the army and the local community and when he is not striding over the Training Area on organised access events John Deighton represents the Swaledale Outdoor Club. The trials, tribulations and triumphs of the farming community are acutely observed and delivered with wry humour by Michael Spensley, the Tenants' representative on the group. Major (Retd) Mark Flecchia, current Training Area Commandant, ensures that a balanced approach is maintained for the wider interests of the Estate users whilst Major (Retd) Martyn Fox ensures that Range safety is maintained to the highest standard. Dick Travell keeps a watchful eye on predation to support the Estate's rich portfolio of wildlife. Stakeholder organisations such as Natural England and the Yorkshire Dales National Park Authority contribute enormously to the meetings and the staff of Landmarc Support Services Ltd, especially Darren East and Josephine Haskett, have facilitated conservation works on the Estate. Last but not least, our gratitude is extended to Sue Snowdon who is the latest in a line of secretaries who have inherited the thankless, but essential, task of taking and distributing the minutes of each meeting.

To everyone, past and present, who have attended and continue to contribute to the Catterick Conservation Group... Thank You.

Defence
Infrastructure
Organisation